The Virtuous Woman: Her Price Is Far Above Rubies

Judy A. Littlejohn

11-10-01

Maria, God bless you
richly as you go to the
next level in God.

Judy Littlejohn

Inspirational Books Enterprise
Randolph, Massachusetts

Unless otherwise indicated, all scriptural quotations are from the *King James Version* of the Bible.

Scripture verses marked NIV are taken from the *New International Version* of the Bible. Copyright © 1973, 1978 by International Bible Society.

The Virtuous Woman: Her Price Is Far Above Rubies
Published by:
Inspirational Books Enterprise
Judy A. Littlejohn, Owner
140 Canton St, Unit E-1
Randolph, MA 02368
ISBN 0-9670791-0-1

Cover design and book production by:
DB & Associates Design Group, Inc.
dba Double Blessing Productions
P.O. Box 52756, Tulsa, OK 74152
www.doubleblessing.com

Printed in the United States of America.

Contents

Acknowledgments

It is in God, that I live, move, and have my being. He is the source and strength of my life. I give Him praise, honor, and glory for what He has done and is doing in my life. I continue to seek His guidance and wisdom that I may please Him and walk in His divine will.

I give honor to my husband, Adam Littlejohn Jr., who supported this project and encouraged me to move forward with it.

I thank God for my mother, Sister Rema McFarling, who continues to encourage me concerning the work of the Lord in my life. She is an inspiration to me. I also thank God for those who contributed their time, skills, abilities, and input toward the start-up and completion of this project. I would like to thank my pastor, Dr. Gwendolyn G. Weeks, for her interest and endorsement of this work. To those of you who had a kind word, wished me well and offered your prayers on behalf of this project, thank you.

To my financial supporters including those who wish to remain anonymous, thank you and may God richly bless you for sowing into this ministry. I express a heartfelt appreciation and gratitude to each of you for your act of kindness.

Sister Ruth Loving Botts, Mr. Daniel S. Cheever, Jr., Minister Charles and Sister LaDonna Christian, Brother Adam B. Littlejohn, Jr., Sister Rema McFarling, Sister Gretchen Saalbach, Ms. Susan Stasiowski, Minister Etlyn B. Steele, Sister Jenese D. Tucker, Minister Hilary G. White.

Foreword

I've had a desire to write books for a few years now (since 1988 to be exact), but hesitated to move forward with this desire. Over the years, I put my writings aside — in a nice folder — to sit on my bookshelf and collect dust. In reading the Word of God and conducting my own personal study of the Bible, I found myself getting topic ideas or "headlines," that could be further developed into story lines.

God re-awakened the desire of my heart to write in early June, 1998. The only way I can describe this re-awakening is by saying that I felt a release in my spirit to make my "dream" a reality. My desire to write was aroused during a Christian Education program at my church one Friday night. The program gave those in attendance an opportunity to share their dreams, goals and desires. As I stood up to share my desire to one day become an author, I re-visited and uncovered a desire that was hidden deep in my heart and knew, almost immediately, that I would move forward this time and not let that desire remain unfruitful in my heart. This particular experience, among others, taught me something that I would like to share with you and that is, whenever you go to the house of God, go with an open mind and with expectation because you never know what God is going to do in you.

Today, I have no regrets about not moving forward in this arena sooner because I believe there is a time and season for everything. I also believe that I had to go through a certain process in order to arrive where I am now. I believe that it is never too late for one to recognize God's purpose in his or her life and act on it as God leads. It is out of this belief that I step out on God's Word according to His plan and purpose for my life. I believe it is time!

It is important for my readers to understand that I do not take this work lightly, nor do I look at it as just an opportunity for me to become an author. Rather, my overall goal and purpose is to reach out to believers — breaking through denominational barriers — and speak to their conditions, situations, fears, doubts, and such like. I intend to do so through the unique way that God has given me to incorporate His Word along with my personal experiences, and the knowledge and wisdom He has given me.

In addition, it is my intent through this book to empower Christian women, letting them know that they are the workmanship of God, regardless of their color, background, denomination, age, or status. Our differences and challenges do not negate the fact that God made us after His likeness and as it pleased Him. The word "different" or "difference" takes on a positive spin in this book because I firmly believe that it is time for us to see our differences as an opportunity and advantage in building up the body of Christ. My desire is that every Christian woman — after reading this book — would appreciate, re-gain, and embrace her self-worth. My purpose is to help Christian women move out from the "surface" and launch out into the "deep" things of God.

Every component of this book is an important contribution toward the continued growth of Christian women.

Pray for me as I move forward in the things of God.

Chapter 1
The Virtuous Woman

Proverbs 31:10-31 portrays the attributes, qualities, and characteristics of a godly or righteous woman. It is apparent that these verses do not describe just any woman; but rather, they describe a woman that is "different," "unique," and "set apart" from the average woman.

When reading verses 10-31 it almost seems impossible that such a woman could exist but the mere fact that these verses were included as a part of the Holy Bible and of Proverbs 31 says to me that such women already do — and can — exist. We know that Scripture is given for our learning, self-edification, and spiritual growth, and we can therefore look at the virtuous woman of Proverbs 31 as a role model for Christian women today.

I believe that as women of God, we can maintain a godly standard in a crooked and perverse world. It is our godly standards that will make a positive impact on those we come in contact with on a daily basis, just as the virtuous woman of Proverbs 31 impacted those in her surroundings. We must stand for righteous living according to the Word of God and the world must be able to see Christ in us in some shape, form, or fashion. In addition, our moral standards must be in line with what the Word of God speaks about us.

This chapter describes the qualities, attributes, and characteristics of the virtuous woman and shows they speak to a broad range of women. It highlights the things that

1

qualifies women to be termed "virtuous" and, at the same time, encourages Christian women that within them lies the potential to become virtuous. I believe that many Christian women already possess virtuous attributes but perhaps do not recognize them as such. By the time you get to the end of this chapter, you will be able to identify things about the virtuous woman of Proverbs 31 that exist in your life and be ready to develop them further, shape them, and move forward in those areas.

I would like to also point out that although these verses are describing the ideal wife and mother, single women and single mothers can also possess some, if not all, of these attributes.

The Virtuous Woman

Who can find a virtuous woman? for her price is far above rubies.

The heart of her husband doth safely trust in her, so that he shall have no need of spoil.

She will do him good and not evil all the days of her life.

She seeketh wool, and flax, and worketh willingly with her hands.

She is like the merchants' ships; she bringeth her food from afar.

She riseth also while it is yet night, and giveth meat to her household, and a portion to her maidens.

She considereth a field, and buyeth it: with the fruit of her hands she planteth a vineyard.

She girdeth her loins with strength, and strengtheneth her arms.

She perceiveth that her merchandise is good: her candle goeth not out by night.

She layeth her hands to the spindle, and her hands hold the distaff.

She stretcheth out her hand to the poor; yea, she reacheth forth her hands to the needy.

She is not afraid of the snow for her household: for all her household are clothed with scarlet.

She maketh herself coverings of tapestry; her clothing is silk and purple.

Her husband is known in the gates, when he sitteth among the elders of the land.

She maketh fine linen, and selleth it; and delivereth girdles unto the merchant.

Strength and honour are her clothing; and she shall rejoice in time to come.

She openeth her mouth with wisdom; and in her tongue is the law of kindness.

She looketh well to the ways of her household, and eateth not the bread of idleness.

Her children arise up, and call her blessed; her husband also, and he praiseth her.

Many daughters have done virtuously, but thou excellest them all.

Favour is deceitful, and beauty is vain: but a woman that feareth the Lord, she shall be praised.

Give her of the fruit of her hands; and let her own works praise her in the gates.

Proverbs 31:10-31

Let's take a closer look at the virtuous woman by examining the following words which *respectively* describe and encompass her.

Virtuous — *"Morally good. Chaste."*[1]

Chaste — *"Morally pure."*[2] *Abstaining from sexual activity.*

Moral — *"Of or concerned with the discernment or instruction of what is good and evil. Being or acting in accordance with established standards of good behavior."*[3]

Noble — *"Having or showing qualities of high moral character."*[4]

Righteous — *"Morally right; just."*[5]

The virtuous woman is righteous. She is justified or "declared righteous" through the shed blood of Jesus. So even where there is sin, upon her acceptance of Christ — through repentance, water baptism, and the in-filling of the Holy Spirit — and obedience to God's Word, she now stands in God's presence sin-free and guilt-free.

First and foremost, her life is centered around a reverent fear of God. She honors and respects God. This says a lot about the virtuous woman. It means that she only wants what God wants, and she plans and organizes her life around God's divine will not only for her, but for her family as well.

The virtuous woman is concerned about doing what is right not only in the eyes of God, but also as it relates to relationships with others, obeying the laws of the land, and possessing and portraying ethical soundness.

The virtuous woman is chaste, not only in conduct but in thought. According to the definition we just read about "chaste," this could be one who is a virgin, or a married, or widowed woman who obviously isn't a virgin, but is morally pure. Not only is God looking for women who will keep themselves from sexual activity outside of marriage, but He's looking for those who have the mind of Christ, those whose consciences have been cleansed from dead works or sin. The single woman must preserve her chastity and the married woman should only indulge in sexual activity within the bonds of her marriage relationship to her husband.

The virtuous woman is exalted above rubies. This is due to her noble character and excellent nature and because she is godly and righteous. Verse 10 of Proverbs 31 emphatically states that "...her price is far above rubies." In other words, she is worth more than earthly riches. The attributes of a virtuous woman means having more worth than material wealth and riches. It is interesting to me that this woman is compared to rubies and therefore, I present the following facts about rubies.

- A ruby is a rare gem.
- Its color is always red.
- It is the second hardest gemstone after the diamond, but its value far exceeds that of a comparable diamond.
- It is the most expensive of all precious gems.
- It is durable, able to exist for a long period of time without significant deterioration.
- It is brilliant.
- It gives a lifetime of satisfaction.

Some other facts that I researched about rubies are that they are bright, striking, distinctive, and radiant. My sister in Christ, I've presented all of these facts to let you know how precious you are in God's sight. The virtuous woman is bright because she glows with the presence of God. She is striking and remarkable. She is unusual, extraordinary, and noteworthy. She is distinctive, different, and her impression is captivating. She is radiant; beaming with the wisdom of God. This woman is secure and confident in whom she is because she's confident in God.

I want to challenge the women of God to embrace their differences. We are all unique according to God's design of our character. How many times have you struggled, perhaps hurting inside because of your desire to be accepted by others, your desire to "fit in?" *Understand that it is not God's will for us all to be alike.* He wants each of us to be uniquely shaped by Him. Realize that it is okay to be different. Remember, God has given gifts according to what is pleasing to Him, and He has instinctively placed skills, abilities, and talents within each of us.

God intended for our differences to be used to build each other up and to contribute to each other's spiritual and natural growth. When we try to model ourselves after someone else, we lose the essence of what God intended us to be to the degree that our own characteristics are hidden. The only one we should strive to be like is our Lord and Savior, Jesus Christ. The Apostle Paul speaks about being "different" as it pertains to gifts and administrations in the body of Christ. Let's take a look.

> **If the foot shall say, Because I am not the hand, I am not of the body; is it therefore not of the body?**
>
> **And if the ear shall say, Because I am not the eye, I am not of the body; is it therefore not of the body?**
>
> **If the whole body were an eye, where were the hearing? If the whole were hearing, where were the smelling?**
>
> **1 Corinthians 12:15-17**

When we can embrace our differences and use them to benefit the body of Christ, then we know that we have reached spiritual maturity.

Do you get the picture? God has placed every member in His body as is fitting. Begin to look at your differences as opportunities not casualties; because a virtuous woman is different, she is distinctive.

She possesses wisdom because she fears God. This wisdom is not tied into intelligence or vast knowledge, but rather is directly related to the fear of the Lord. Now let's take a look at some of the writings of Proverbs about wisdom.

> **"Get wisdom, get understanding; do not forget my words or swerve from them.**
>
> **"Do not forsake wisdom, and *she will protect you; love her, and she will watch over you.***
>
> **"Wisdom is supreme; therefore get wisdom. Though it cost all you have, get understanding.**
>
> **"Esteem her, and she will exalt you; embrace her, and she will honor you.**
>
> **"She will set a garland of grace on your head and present you with a crown of splendor."**
>
> **Proverbs 4:5-9 (NIV)**

Godly wisdom is essential for a meaningful, godly life. In the life of a virtuous woman, wisdom is important to seek after. It must be sought out above all things. Wisdom comes through, and can be attained by following (or obeying) godly instructions. It comes to believers who have a sincere relationship with God and to those who reverently fear the Lord.

Wisdom is a life-giving source. One who embraces godly wisdom will live as God has designed him or her to live, experience a good, joyful and long life and, live a moral and spiritual life.

Wisdom will guard one's heart. Proverbs 4:23 tells us that the heart is the wellspring of life. It is the place where our desires and decisions are contemplated and made. We generally consider the brain to be the center and director of human activity, yet the Bible, according to the NIV, speaks of the heart as the "center" or wellspring of life.

> He [Jesus] went on: "What comes out of a man is what makes him 'unclean.'
>
> "For from within, out of men's hearts, come evil thoughts, sexual immorality, theft, murder, adultery,
>
> "greed, malice, deceit, lewdness, envy, slander, arrogance and folly.
>
> "All these evils come from inside and make a man 'unclean.'"
>
> Mark 7:20-23 (NIV)

In essence, these verses are saying that sin proceeds (comes from) the heart (see also Matthew 12:34). The heart is the center of the intellect, the center of the emotions, and the center of human will. An impure heart will, in fact, corrupt one's thoughts, feelings, words, and actions. It is in the heart of an individual that God speaks. In fact, Psalm 95:7,8 (NIV) says "...Today, if you hear his voice, do not harden your hearts as you did at Meribah...." Where will you hear His voice? In your heart.

Wisdom will help you to move in the direction that God is taking you and at the same time cause you to recognize, understand, and know how to use the resources God has placed in your hands, in your home, on your job, in your surroundings and community. Wisdom will preserve you; it will spare you from making unnecessary mistakes and bad decisions. King Solomon, for example, had wisdom because *he asked God for it*. Wisdom gave him direction in leading the people, gave him favor with people, made him prosperous, and added stability and soundness to his decision-making in terms of being a leader. My sister, you have that same wisdom available to you today. All you have to do is ask God for it.

If any of you lacks wisdom, he should ask God, who gives generously to all without finding fault, and it will be given to him.

But when he asks, he must believe and not doubt, because he who doubts is like a wave of the sea, blown and tossed by the wind.
                                              James 1:5,6 (NIV)

So you see, the key to the virtuous woman's success is godly wisdom and a reverent fear of God. She possesses a strong, consistent, and stable relationship with God. In the natural realm, building relationships takes much work. It takes giving of yourself and receiving of others. It takes sharing, trusting, caring, loving, listening, correcting, giving space, and so on. In the spiritual realm, it takes the same effort and more to develop a relationship with God. The difference with God is that He is our creator so He knows all about us, and we can trust Him. He won't look down on us. He won't speak badly about us. He will forgive us, and the list goes on. What a compassionate, caring God we serve!

The following are three major areas of a virtuous woman that *respectively* contribute to her overall make up.

1. **Godly Characteristics.**

2. **Responsibility, Position, and Contribution to Husband.**

3. **Contributions to Family and Society.**

Godly Characteristics

A virtuous woman fears God and centers the affairs of her life around pleasing Him. She doesn't move out on her own but seeks and acknowledges God in every area of her life. Godly wisdom is the fuel that drives her, and God is her motivator.

A virtuous woman seeks God continually. Understandably one cannot always be in the posture of prayer (kneeling) as we know it, but one can maintain a prayerful attitude; such is the virtuous woman. She prays on behalf of her household and others. She understands that consistent communication with God is vital to her existence.

A virtuous woman girds herself with spiritual strength in order to carry out her God-given tasks. She prays, studies the Bible, fasts, and assembles herself regularly with God's people to contribute to the edification and perfecting of the saints.

A virtuous woman involves herself in the things of God publicly and privately.

A virtuous woman is earnest and sincere in her doings. When she does for others, it's not out of selfish motive, but it is sincere and well-meaning.

The single *virtuous* woman's mind is continually on the things of God and how she can please Him. Because she continually meditates on Him, she is kept in perfect peace (Isaiah 26:3).

However, the virtuous woman knows that because she is a godly woman, there is an attack against her by Satan. She knows that the forces of evil are just as real as God Himself, but not more powerful than God. She realizes that her own wisdom, intellect and earthly possessions cannot successfully defeat the attacks of the devil. So she clothes herself in righteousness on a daily basis. As women of God, we too must clothe ourselves daily according to Ephesians 6:11-18. Let's take a look.

Put on the whole armor of God, that ye may be able to stand against the wiles of the devil.

For we wrestle not against flesh and blood, but against principalities, against powers, against the rulers of the darkness of this world, against spiritual wickedness in high places.

Wherefore take unto you the whole armor of God, that ye may be able to withstand in the evil day, and having done all, to stand.

Stand therefore, having your loins girt about with truth, and having on the breastplate of righteousness;

And your feet shod with the preparation of the gospel of peace;

Above all, taking the shield of faith, wherewith ye shall be able to quench all the fiery darts of the wicked.

And take the helmet of salvation, and the sword of the Spirit, which is the word of God:

Praying always with all prayer and supplication in the Spirit, and watching thereunto with all perseverance and supplication for all saints.

The "whole armor" is the virtuous woman's attire because she understands "spiritual warfare." She appreciates and utilizes every protective covering that God has given her to fight against the enemy. She is familiar with the schemes of the enemy because she studies them through the Word of God.

As women of God, understanding spiritual warfare is important to our spiritual growth and success as well as our overall defeat of the enemy. Therefore I would like to deviate for a moment and present this next section on the whole armor as it pertains to spiritual warfare.

The Whole Armor: Spiritual Warfare

There are three major themes in Ephesians 6:11-18. First, we are living in the evil day. Second, we will engage in spiritual warfare. Third, we must put on the whole armor of God.

We are instructed as believers to take the whole armor of God that we may be able to *withstand* in the evil day. The word "withstand" means, in part, "to stand against: resist; to oppose successfully."[6] James tells us to "resist the devil, and he will flee from you" (James 4:7). The only way that we can successfully withstand the devil is with the Word of God, our sword.

God's Word must be in our mouths, and we must meditate on it day and night to observe to do according to *all* that is written therein. It is only then that we will make our way prosperous and experience good success according to Joshua 1:8. God's Word must be a part of our spiritual diet. Let's look at some of the key words — and their definitions and/or descriptions — used in Ephesians 6:11-18.

> **Stand** — "To take or be at rest in an upright position. To remain stationary or unchanged. To be steadfast."[7]

> **Armor** — "Protective covering."[8] A defensive covering worn to protect the body. Something that protects or defends.

In the natural realm, one dresses according to the seasons or according to the weather conditions of one's particular geographical location. For example, during the spring and summer lighter clothing is worn but during the fall and winter heavier clothing is worn. For what purpose? To cover, conceal, or protect the body against the elements of nature and to give privacy from others. The same rule applies in the spiritual sense. The one who does not clothe himself/herself spiritually will not be protected from the fiery darts of the enemy. Let us look at some of the components that make up our spiritual armor. These components will be defined in the natural realm, but we know that our armor is spiritual.

> **Shield** — "A broad piece of defensive armor carried on the arm. Something that protects or hides."[9] There were two kinds of shields used during the Bible days.

1. The large shield encompassed the whole person and was used only when not in actual conflict. It was carried in front of the warrior.

2. A smaller shield was used in hand-to-hand fighting. This shield was called the buckler or target.

In actual conflict one needs to be free in movement, not weighted down. Therefore the smaller shield would be more ideal to use in hand-to-hand combat. In spiritual warfare, the shield of faith is mandatory for all believers at all times.

In the spiritual realm, I believe the shield of faith encompasses the whole person as well as serves a distinct purpose in actual conflict. As I examined the word "faith," I found that it acts as a stimulus for the believer. In other words, faith excites the believer to action. Faith without works is dead, according to James 2:17. Your faith in God and in His Word will produce works. Hearing and applying the Word of God to your life will also produce faith (Romans 10:17).

Helmet — "A protective covering for the head."[10] The covering is made of metal. In the Bible days, the covering was also made of leather or plastic.

The helmet of salvation protects the mind of the believer and though Satan launches his attacks, they will not be successful nor will they prosper.

We know, according to Isaiah 54:17, that no weapon formed against us will prosper. My sister in Christ, defeat begins in the mind. If Satan can successfully penetrate and bombard your mind with doubt, fear, paranoia, and unbelief, then he has defeated you! What you need to do is read and confess — on a daily basis — Scriptures that address the protection of the mind through Christ. Scriptures such as Isaiah 26:3,4 which says that the one whose mind is stayed on God will be kept in perfect peace; Philippians 2:5, you must have the mind of Christ; 2 Timothy 1:7, God has given you the spirit of sanity or a sound mind; and Philippians 4:6,7, the peace of God will keep your heart and mind through Christ Jesus. Faithful and consistent confession of — and belief in — these Scriptures will deliver your mind from the attacks of the enemy.

Breastplate — "A metal plate of armor for the breast."[11] It was worn to protect the front of the body (chest area). In Scripture, it is referred to as "a coat of mail" (1 Samuel 17:5).

The fact that Christ has made us righteous, morally right, or just, is the protection that guards our heart which is the center of our being. Our own righteousness — which is as filthy rags — cannot put us in right standing with God (Isaiah 64:6).

Sword — "A weapon with a long blade for cutting or thrusting."[12]

Our sword is the Word of God.

For the word of God is living and active. Sharper than any double-edged sword, it penetrates even to dividing soul and spirit, joint and marrow; it judges the thoughts and attitudes of the heart.
Hebrews 4:12 (NIV)

Remember, our fight is not against flesh and blood. It is spiritual warfare against the kingdom of Satan. Spiritual armor and weapons are used in spiritual warfare just as physical armor and weapons are used in physical combat.

For though we live in the world, we do not wage war as the world does.

The weapons we fight with are not the weapons of the world. On the contrary, they have divine power to demolish strongholds.

We demolish arguments and every pretension that sets itself up against the knowledge of God, and we take captive every thought to make it obedient to Christ.
2 Corinthians 10:3-5 (NIV)

One may try to use earthly knowledge and wisdom to fight against the devil but these are in themselves inadequate to pull down Satan's strongholds. We cannot fight Satan with earthly weapons. We must fight him with spiritual weapons. Fighting the attacks of Satan with earthly weapons will only defeat and devastate the believer! It is only by the Word of God and by putting on our spiritual armor that we can fight against the attacks of Satan. Satan's attempt is to hold as many people as he can in the clutches of sin. Sin has a grip that only the power of God can destroy. The church's weapons should be faith, righteousness, the power of the Holy Spirit, and the Word of God.

Here are some weapons or tools that are key to the believer's victory in warfare.

- Prayer
- Worship
- Praise
- Singing
- Shouting
- Dancing
- Meditation on God's Word
- Confession of and belief in God's Word

Putting on the whole armor of God along with these other tools sets the tone for victory and changes the atmosphere around you. This means that we must live up to the standard of God's Word. We can't live shabby lives as Christians — "one foot in the church and the other foot in the world" — and expect God to come to our rescue. God requires holiness. He expects us to be consistent and to progress in our daily walk with Him.

Here are some helpful tips for engaging in spiritual warfare:

1. Don't verbalize the method of attack or strategy that you will use against the enemy. Discuss your warfare strategy or plan of attack with your commander, God. However, learn to do so in the Spirit or your "prayer language." In plain words, pray in

tongues! When you pray in tongues in a private sense, only God can interpret what you are saying and you edify yourself (1 Corinthians 14:4).

Your warfare against Satan's spiritual forces calls for an intensity in prayer. You will experience a great sense of relief and victory in the "heat of the battle" when you pray in tongues.

It is important, however, that you don't abuse tongues. In addition, be aware that some non-Christian religions, under the influence of Satan, practice tongues, but it is not of God! Tongues must come from God "as the Spirit wills," not as you will. Don't play with tongues nor use it under false pretense. You will end up in more trouble than you bargained for! You should speak in tongues "as the Spirit of God gives you utterance" (Acts 2:3,4; 10:44-46, 1 Corinthians 14:15).

2. You can't be a coward! If you are going to engage in spiritual warfare, and you will, you must realize your warfare potential, be familiar with and know how to use every spiritual weapon available to you, and be ready and willing to fight against the forces of evil.

3. Natural intellect won't help you in spiritual combat. You must use your spiritual intellect; put on the mind of Christ, the helmet of salvation.

You must know that God is your hiding place and that He will compass you about with songs of deliverance (Psalm 32:7).

Jehoshaphat became fearful when he received word that a great multitude was against him. He immediately sought the Lord and proclaimed a fast throughout Judah. God sent word through Jahaziel that Jehoshaphat should not fear nor be dismayed by reason of the great multitude, because the battle belonged to God (2 Chronicles 20:15-17, 21,22).

Satan will try to intimidate you by using numbers and size, but God is not moved by numbers or size! Didn't

God tell Gideon to get rid of all the fearful men from his army? There were too many men in Gideon's army for God to deliver the Midianites into their hands. Gideon's army was reduced from 32,000 to 300 (Judges 7:2-8). Only God's presence and activity can ensure victory for His people. God is looking for those who are dedicated to Him to show them that it's not by might, nor by power, but by His Spirit (Zechariah 4:6). Spiritual alertness and dedication is what counts, not numbers.

Jehoshaphat received instruction of what his profile should be during battle, and we should have the same profile.

- Set yourself — prepare and position yourself for battle;

- Stand still and see — don't waiver, don't run, don't let the enemy intimidate you;

- Fear not, nor be dismayed — don't panic, don't become anxious or apprehensive;

- Go out against them — move forward; face your enemy.

Jehoshaphat even appointed singers unto the Lord to praise the beauty of His holiness. A song of praise and victory is a powerful tool in warfare! Many times in Scripture, songs of praise preceded God's people into battle and brought total defeat on the enemy through the power of God. *Sometimes* the Word of God and a song of praise will be your only — but most powerful and effective — weapons against the attacks of the enemy. You cannot become discouraged because it seems like nothing is happening on your behalf. Victory is not always in sight, but if you follow God's instructions, you will come out on top.

Satan is after those who will make an uncompromising stand for the Gospel of Jesus Christ. His attack is primarily in three areas:

1. The Christian.
2. The home.
3. The church.

Satan is filled with fury and his anger is directed at God and His people. Knowing this, it is imperative that the believer does not underestimate, or take lightly, the power of Satan. That's why the Word of God admonishes us to "Be sober, be vigilant; because your adversary the devil, as a roaring lion, walketh about, seeking whom he may devour" (1 Peter 5:8). Be alert. Know what's going on around you.

As I close out this section on spiritual warfare to continue with more in-depth descriptions and attributes of a virtuous woman, it is important that you understand that warfare occurs when your opponent (the adversary) desires to pull you down out of the place or position God has placed you in. He wants to publicly humiliate and embarrass you so that he can be seen as the victor. However, Romans 8:37 declares that you are more than a conqueror through Christ that loves you.

As I continue now with the first major area of a virtuous woman — Godly Characteristics — I'm sure that you already see that a virtuous woman's interest is gaining the mind of Christ. Why? Because she knows that the carnal or "worldly" mind is hostile against the things of God. In fact, it cannot even receive the things of God (Romans 8:7). More importantly, the virtuous woman knows that "...to be carnally minded is death; but to be spiritually minded is life and peace" (Romans 8:6). This is important to her since she is striving for eternal life with Christ. The virtuous woman brings her mind in subjection to the law of God by renewing it daily with the Word of God. This way she ensures that she does not conform to the things of this world but instead, is transformed by the renewing of her mind (Romans 12:2). The virtuous woman knows that the Word of God says "Let this mind be in you, which was also in Christ Jesus" (Philippians 2:5). She also understands that she must go beyond just knowing the Word, to being a doer of it (See James 1:22-25).

A virtuous woman works for God with diligence. She serves Him with joy and gladness. She is able to do this because the joy of the Lord is her strength (Nehemiah 8:10). His joy actually gives her spiritual (as well as physical and mental) strength. This kind of joy is not circumstantial because it is not based on things, people, or status. It is a consistent, renewing kind of joy that comes up in the "inner person" regardless of circumstances. It is the kind of joy that far surpasses happiness which is conditional and is based on circumstances, people, things, and earthly accomplishments.

I believe one of the ways we can obtain this joy is given in the Gospel of John 16:24. Our joy rests in our ability to "ask." But even more so in our ability to relate to God and trust that He can and will meet our needs.

A virtuous woman can discern, not only the things of God, but also that which is best for her household. She can detect — perceive with the eye or mind — those things that are good or bad for her family. She can do this because she has built a relationship — through prayer — with God and she knows His Word. Her ability to discern is not based on her own knowledge or wisdom, but it is based on the fact that she is "familiar" with those things that please God.

A virtuous woman strives to guard her tongue as described in Ephesians 4:29 (NIV).

> **Do not let any unwholesome talk come out of your mouths, but only what is helpful for building others up according to their needs, that it may benefit those who listen.**

Our tongue should be used to build up, edify, and strengthen each other, not tear each other down. We are to be very careful in how we use our tongue (See James 3).

A virtuous woman always looks ahead and plans for the future according to God's instruction. She can rejoice in days ahead knowing that she has made preparation for that time. A virtuous woman is never caught off guard. She is always prepared!

As women of God, we must constantly develop our relationship with God, focusing on our inner attributes and beauty as well as our self-esteem. I will briefly address the topic of self-esteem and how we sometimes link it to the outward appearance later in this chapter.

Responsibility, Position, and Contribution to Husband

A virtuous woman comforts her husband. In times of discomfort, unrest, and indecision, she brings him comfort. She assures him that with the help of God, everything will work together for the good. She also reaffirms her support of him.

A virtuous woman encourages her husband. When he feels like giving up and becomes discouraged, she's a constant friend and source of encouragement to him.

A virtuous woman treats her husband well. She is loving, kind, and respectful to him, and will never do him wrong. She is a crowning joy to him and he has no need to be ashamed of her. In fact, he praises her.

A virtuous woman has a trusting relationship with her husband. She's honest and open with him, sharing her thoughts and desires and listening to his.

A virtuous woman stands ready to assist her husband whenever the need arises. She looks at her position as "help meet" to her husband as an opportunity to help him achieve goals for himself and for the entire family. In other words, she is a constant and consistent resource to him. She is prudent in business dealings. She is cautious, discreet, and sensible. She does not deal crookedly or dishonestly in financial matters or business negotiations. She makes wise investments that will benefit her family, and she uses *her* monetary substance to start new ventures. The virtuous woman of Proverbs 31 saw a field (or vineyard) that had "good ground." In other words, the soil was good and it was suitable to invest in for business. So she purchased it with her own money. She then planted grapevines — which produced grapes — for her family, and she probably sold some to the merchants for the marketplace.

A virtuous woman is never idle but always occupied serving God, her family, and others, and developing herself to be a better person. It is a pleasure for her to use the skills, talents, and abilities that God has given her. There's no time for her to sit by idly; she's too busy! Her mind is well occupied and there's no room for her to entertain ungodly or unfruitful thoughts. I must add, however, that although the virtuous woman keeps herself busy with the things of God and going about her daily tasks, she knows how to take full advantage of getting rest and relaxation — which is a part of God's plan — as needed. She knows that rest is important to her mental, physical, and spiritual state of being. We refer to such a "rest" as *vacation.*

Although this section dealt with the virtuous woman's responsibility toward her husband, I want to reiterate the fact that single women can exemplify virtuous attributes as well in many other ways. For example, a woman doesn't have to be married in order to know how to encourage herself or her children in the things of God and life in general. In fact, single Christian women are at a greater advantage than those of us who are married because they can focus on — and give their entire attention more fully to the things of God (See 1 Corinthians 7:34).

Contributions to Family and Society

The virtuous woman is compassionate toward those in need. She is not proud or selfish, but rather uses her accomplishments to help others. She realizes that if it had not been for God on her side, she could not make any progress in life (Psalm 124:1-5).

A virtuous woman works diligently *with purpose* to serve her family and others. She is very focused. One who works with purpose gets more self-gratification than one who just works; because the one with purpose is focused on accomplishing specific tasks in areas that God has called him or her to. For example, it would be a waste of time for one to put all of his or her effort into something that he or she is not capable of doing. One who just cannot sing and lacks potential in this area need not waste time trying to build a career in singing. The more we mature spiritually (and naturally), the more we will desire to spend our time doing the things that God has called us to do, even more so as we become aware of the shortness of time in terms of the rapture of the church.

A virtuous woman works willingly with her hands, volunteering without reluctance. She focuses on the needs of others and how she can encourage and uplift them. It is not a chore for her to serve others, it's an honor because she understands servant-hood. The key is, the more she yields herself to God, the more she can yield herself to others. I must say that servant-hood isn't easy. In order for one to serve others, one must be willing to give of himself or herself freely and unselfishly, even if he or she is taken for granted. In other words, a servant submits to the authority of someone else, giving up all rights. This is not easy for most people to do, nor does it happen overnight! Let's take a closer look at servanthood for a brief moment. After all, it is a very important aspect of our role as Christians.

A servant is one who is willing and able to provide whatever others need in order *to make them complete.* A servant's focus is totally on the other person. The reason many find it difficult to serve — not as though they are incapable of serving — is perhaps because they think there has to be mutual trust and friendship in order to serve others. Well if it was this easy none of us would have a problem serving others. With trust, comes belief in an individual. People like to feel that there is a level of genuine care, respect, and appreciation toward them as they serve others. But this is not always the case. In addition, people want to know that the sacrificing of their time and effort will not be abused or taken for granted as a servant. In other words, servants are often "used." To be used in this sense means to be taken for granted in his/her role (and taken advantage of) by others without any regard for the servant's needs, self-worth, or desires. When it comes to the body of Christ, we must have regard for one another. If not, we will become "burnt out" as servants and less effective in the things God has called us to.

It takes a lot to put the needs of others before your own needs. Whether you are a preacher, teacher, youth leader, administrator, head of the hospitality committee, music director, and so on, one can only truly serve as he or she begins to value the existence of those in the body of Christ as well as those who do not have Christ. In fact, our primary purpose as Christians is to serve those who still remain in sin, by ministering the Gospel of Jesus Christ. We must always remember that Christ reached out and pulled us out of sin because He loves us. By the same token, we must reach out even to our enemies and serve them through the love of God.

In the days we are living in, there is a desperate need for trust, sincerity, and loyalty in the body of Christ. This is not the time to play games with one another. It is not the time to "put on a face" toward one another and then change faces behind each other's back. It is time to treat one another with respect and to love each other without some underlying motive. We don't have to like each other's ways, but we are commanded to love each other because love is of God. In fact, Jesus said the only way others will know that we are His disciples is if we have love one for the other (John 13:35, see also verse 34). *The American Heritage Dictionary* defines "disciple" as "one who accepts the teachings of a master and often assists in spreading them." As Christians we are all commissioned to spread the Gospel throughout the world which puts us in a servant category. So *it isn't "works" alone that define a servant, it's "love"* (a genuine, unconditional feeling expressed toward another). This God-kind of love will even cause us to love our enemies. No one wants a servant who does everything that is asked of him yet does it with a terrible attitude of complaining and murmuring!

If we truly want to become servants of the Lord and servants to each other then we must examine and pattern ourselves after the life of Jesus, Paul, and Timothy, to name a few, all of whom portrayed the life of a *true* servant. See Philippians 2 which lets us know that serving requires a submissive, self-less mind. In this chapter, Christ is depicted as a servant.

Let's get back to the virtuous woman's contributions to family and society. A virtuous woman is a servant to her family and she holds her family in high regard. She wants the best for them. In Proverbs 31, the virtuous woman traveled at length to buy food for her household. This indicates a sacrificial kind of care and regard that caused her to do whatever it took to give her family the best.

A virtuous woman welcomes opportunities because they give her a chance to expand and strengthen her skills and abilities as well as gain new ones.

A virtuous woman is an example to her family and to others. She is a woman of her word, a woman of character.

A virtuous woman will ensure that the affairs of her home are conducted in an orderly, godly manner with grace and dignity.

A virtuous woman gives careful thought to every decision before it is made because she doesn't want to be out of the will of God or do something she will ultimately regret. She is not impulsive or quick to act; but rather waits to hear from God and sense peace within herself before she proceeds.

A virtuous woman sees to it that her family is clothed with the best. The virtuous woman in Proverbs 31 was a talented seamstress. She made her family's clothing using the best fabrics and colors of the day. For example, she used scarlet and purple, colors that represented royalty. She also took pride in her appearance. Her own clothes were made of silk. However, a virtuous woman is never trendy, but she develops her own individual style and thus, her own identity. Having said this, I feel obligated to say a few words about outward appearance and self-esteem in the next few paragraphs. Let's break for a moment to address the issue of self-esteem.

In the natural realm, women usually feel better about themselves if their outward appearance is together. We are concerned about how we look; therefore, we make investments in skin care products, health care products, hair treatment products, and clothing and accessories that accentuate our beauty. We often link how we feel inwardly (our self-esteem) to how good we look and dress outwardly. Unfortunately enhancing the outward appearance cannot make one feel better if there are deep-rooted problems that have not been addressed and resolved. The outward appearance provides momentary satisfaction and happiness. Inward problems and issues need to be resolved before one can experience true happiness and peace. Therefore our concentration as women of God should be on the inner person first and then the outer person.

Some women feel that all their problems will go away if they can just "dress them up." In other words, "If I can look better, maybe I will feel better." Sometimes this is true but not in all cases — and only to an extent. By the same token, some women with low self-esteem feel that if they can look good in the eyes of others (e.g., husband or friends), they will feel better about themselves. This may be true for some women to a degree, but Christian women should learn to please God first, and not only seek to please others. In addition, it's important that we feel good about ourselves and about how we look. We *should be* beautiful for ourselves, and the real beauty starts within. Someone best described this inner beauty as a kind of beauty you can cultivate that will not fade over the years. I must caution that women (men also) can become vain in trying to beautify themselves outwardly if they become "materialistic" and begin to put all their focus on "looks." In fact, Proverbs 31:30 says "Favour is deceitful, and beauty is vain: but a woman that feareth the Lord, she shall be praised." What I'm trying to say is that there should be balance in our lives.

In the spiritual realm, a true Spirit-filled woman will already glow with the light of Christ. She must continue to "put on Christ" daily, and as she does this, she will be built up with confidence and assurance in God. This is what's so intriguing about the virtuous woman. She has inner beauty, confidence in God, self-worth, and self-esteem. If you take care of your inner person, you will glow!

Feeling good about being a woman of God will do wonders in lifting your spirits. The inability to recognize and accept yourself as God created you will bring grief to your spirit. God does not want you to be grieved. He wants you to know that everything *He* created was good from the beginning of time. That means you!

Satan's job is to make you feel unhappy, tense, anxious, stressed out, depressed, and angry about things you can't change by your own power. If you fill yourself with God's love and walk in His Word, His presence will calm your spirit. I hope this section on self-esteem helps you to identify and come to grips with where *your* self-esteem is, or rather should be rooted. I think this is an area we can all either identify with or work on to some degree or another.

A virtuous woman maintains her profession and contributes her talents to society. Whether she is in full-time ministry, missions, or evangelism, works for an organization, or is self-employed, she is a blessing to others through the works of her hands, her wisdom, and intellect. The virtuous woman depicted in Proverbs 31 was an entrepreneur who made fine linen garments for wholesale in the marketplace.

She maketh fine linen, and selleth it; and delivereth girdles unto the merchant.
Proverbs 31:24

A virtuous woman never stops learning. She sees her experiences as a way to learn more and strive for better.

A virtuous woman is courageous. She walks by faith, trusting in God. This kind of woman will be rewarded by God — and recognized by others — for the things done to bring glory to Him. Although her motive is not necessarily to be rewarded by others, her faithfulness to God causes her to be recognized by others. Her works will be a testimony of her nobility throughout the city.

A virtuous woman, however, is not just virtuous because of her *attributes,* it is her *attitude* towards God, her family and others, as well as how she sees herself. Spirituality is essential to this woman. She possesses an inner calm and confidence that comes from her relationship with God.

Finally, a virtuous woman is aware that there is always potential for growth and continues to strive toward that end, trusting in the Lord. Her weaknesses pose no threat to her because her God is greater. She possesses the strength to overcome all things through Christ Jesus (1 John 4:4, Romans 8:37, Philippians 4:13).

As I close out this chapter, it is my hope and desire that we realize God has given each of us talents and abilities that are not contingent on anyone else. For example, in looking at the virtuous woman in Proverbs 31, it is obvious that she "carried her own weight." This woman was remarkable! She caught people's attention no matter where she went or what she did — even though she wasn't seeking it. There was something very captivating about the way in which she carried herself, the way she served God, and the way she served others. I firmly believe that it was because of her notable deeds that her husband was known in the city. As a matter of fact, her husband praised her to others throughout the city. This woman's spiritual and earthly success was contingent on God alone. She was notable because she yielded to God, and because of this her family called her blessed (Proverbs 31:28).

You may ask, "How do we become virtuous women?" My personal conviction and advice to women is, "The more you surrender to God, the more you become like Him and the less you remain yourself." This way there is little or no space for you to shape yourself. As women in the body of Christ, we must begin to speak, believe, and live the words of John 3:30 (NIV), "He must become greater; I [we] must become less."

Don't feel disheartened because you may not possess all of the qualities of a virtuous woman. You would be a rare find if you did! Individually, we may not possess *all* of the attributes of a virtuous woman, but each of us possesses some of those attributes. The key is to serve God, your family, and others with the ability and material resources that God has given you. All of us, put together, become the virtuous woman — as a body, as we come together, all the attributes are reflected.

I believe that we need to build on our strengths as a body until we become one representation of a "virtuous woman." That means pulling all of our resources together to benefit the body of Christ. Our strengths may vary in areas such as organizational skills, coordination of programs and events, teaching, preaching, musical abilities, hospitality, and so on. Whatever our strengths, it will benefit the church better if our efforts are more collective. You have a place, women of God! Whatever you can offer in the work of the Lord is needed in the body of Christ.

It is my hope and prayer that this chapter has given you more insight into Proverbs 31. I trust that you have been enlightened and your perspective has been broadened so that you can go forth as a virtuous woman of God.

[1] *The American Heritage Dictionary* (Houghton Mifflin Company, 1983), p. 759.
[2] *The American Heritage Dictionary*, p. 118.
[3] *The American Heritage Dictionary*, p. 444.
[4] *The American Heritage Dictionary*, p. 463.
[5] *The American Heritage Dictionary*, p. 593.
[6] *The Merriam Webster Dictionary* (Philippines: Merriam-Webster, Inc., 1994), p. 845.
[7] *The Merriam Webster Dictionary*, p. 703.
[8] *The Merriam Webster Dictionary*, p. 56.
[9] *The Merriam Webster Dictionary*, p. 669.
[10] *The Merriam Webster Dictionary*, p. 347.
[11] *The Merriam Webster Dictionary*, p. 104.
[12] *The Merriam Webster Dictionary*, p. 729.

Chapter 2
Their Lives Still Speak

In this section, I want to take a look at some of the women in the Bible who show some of the attributes of a virtuous woman. I have selected these women to profile as God placed them on my heart. I have highlighted the attributes and qualities that made them virtuous. We can learn something from each one of these women. I have covered attributes in each woman that we can relate to as 21st Century women of God. These women are depicted in this chapter in a very unique way. Many of you will see a mirror of yourself in the lives of these women.

Hannah: A Woman of Prayer and Integrity

Pray: "To utter or address a prayer to a deity. To make a fervent request for something."[1]

Integrity: "Strict personal honesty and independence. Completeness; unity. Soundness."[2]

We read about Hannah in First and Second Samuel. She was the wife of Elkanah — his favorite wife — and the woman who eventually became the mother of Samuel. Hannah remained prayerful during a time when her circumstances and surroundings were not conducive to prayer. Immorality was prevalent in the land, and there was no regard for the house of God. Eli's two sons Hophni and Phinehas met up with "temple prostitutes" at the entrance of the temple in Shiloh. This was the same temple that Hannah and Elkanah traveled to, yearly to worship God. The

Israelites had strayed from the standards set forth by God and eventually shifted from a theocracy in which God was their only King to a democracy. During this time, Hannah could have turned from God, but she remained focused knowing that her help was in God.

Hannah faced a tremendous obstacle — at least it was an obstacle for women during Hannah's days. She was barren and unable to conceive. During those times, it was a shame and disgrace for women to be childless, especially to be without a son. I'm sure that this situation left Hannah feeling distressed and discouraged, especially since Elkanah's other wife Peninnah was able to bear children. Can you imagine how Hannah felt every time she looked around and Peninnah was pregnant? After all, she was Elkanah's wife too, and she wanted to bear his seed. Hannah could have very well become enraged with jealousy and envy; but instead, she trusted in God who was able to perform miracles. I am quite sure that at times Hannah became jealous of Peninnah, but she did not allow jealousy to rule her. She steadfastly sought God year after year.

Hannah was faithful and consistent in her prayers to God. She had to believe that God would open her womb; otherwise she would not have traveled year after year to the temple at Shiloh to petition God. I'm sure that Hannah prayed about other things, but knowing that her greatest test was her inability to conceive, she placed this request at the top of her prayer list. This test was always before her as she observed other families journeying to Shiloh with their little ones. This must have been difficult for Hannah, yet Hannah's faith remained strong.

Although, Hannah was barren, and had no children to care for, Elkanah gave her a "double portion" of meat because he loved her and probably felt sorry for her because the Lord had closed her womb. He probably felt that he needed to make up to her, in some way, for what she didn't have (1 Samuel 1:4,5). To make matters worse, Peninnah mocked and made fun of Hannah because she could not conceive. Now imagine, Peninnah was jealous of Hannah because she was Elkanah's favorite wife. That's why she mocked her for being barren. It seem to me that Hannah should have been the jealous one, picking at Peninnah out of jealousy. Women of God, if you spend time seeking God and His divine will (which is revealed in His Word) and His purpose for your life, you will have no time to be jealous or envious of anyone else.

With God on your side, you have more going for you than you know. That is why Satan picks at you!

As time went on, Hannah became very grieved over the matter and finally reached a "breaking point." As at other times, she poured out her heart before God. She still knew that only God could help her. Truly Hannah's prayer life reflected the words of James 5:16, "...The effectual fervent prayer of a righteous man [person] availeth much."

Hannah's Prayer

And she vowed a vow, and said, O Lord of hosts, if thou wilt indeed look on the affliction of thine handmaid, and remember me, and not forget thine handmaid, but wilt give unto thine handmaid a man child, then I will give him unto the Lord all the days of his life, and there shall no razor come upon his head.

1 Samuel 1:11

Hannah promised God that if He gave her a son, she would dedicate this child back to Him. Later on, we find out that God opened Hannah's womb, and she kept her word to God. People often make promises to God based on their needs, but when He comes through, the promises are not kept. Hannah was not like this. She was a woman of her word.

Hannah's life portrayed humility, submission, and a sense of dependence on God. The Word of God lets us know that if we humble ourselves under the mighty hand of God, He will exalt us in due time (1 Peter 5:6). In a situation that seemed unbearable for Hannah, she knew how to petition

God — she knew how to maintain her composure. Sometimes we pray about things, and it doesn't seem like anything is going to happen. But hold on, be persistent with God, and wait on Him; He will come through for you.

Finally, God answered Hannah's prayer, and she conceived a son and called his name Samuel which means "asked of the Lord" (1 Samuel 1:20). Hannah truly was a virtuous woman. She exhibited a prayer life that was not disrupted by circumstances. Hannah not only prayed in the bad times, but she continued to pray when things got better. Because Hannah kept her promise to God concerning Samuel and had faith in Him, He blessed her with more children — more than she originally asked for.

I believe there are four things that worked for Hannah's advantage:

1. Hannah *went* to the place where God promised to meet His people.
2. She *went* to the place of offering.
3. She *entered* the place of worship.
4. She *exposed* herself in the house of prayer.

Hannah continued worshipping God at the set time and place (the temple at Shiloh). In other words, she maintained her devotions. Yes, Hannah's affliction brought her to her knees, but her consistency in prayer caused her to get the one thing she desired most from God, a son.

Ruth: The Woman Who Loved

> **Love:** "Intense affection and warm feeling for another."[3]

Ruth was a foreigner from the land of Moab, located east of the Dead Sea. She was married to Mahlon, son of Naomi. Ruth was known as a "stranger" because she was amongst a people who were not her own (unlike Naomi, a Jew from Bethlehem-Judah). Ruth was Naomi's daughter-in-law, and she possessed an enduring, undying love for her mother-in-law. What an attribute! Her friendship and loyalty to Naomi was unique.

Because of Ruth's dedication to Naomi, the people of Bethlehem admired and favored her. They noticed something "different" about this Moabite woman. She was loving, gentle, humble, sweet, and kind.

Ruth became a widow at a young age and could have separated herself from her husband's family, but she didn't. It was obvious that Ruth loved Mahlon because even after his death, she remained loyal to his mother, their people, their country, and their God.

> **And Ruth said, Entreat me not to leave thee, or to return from following after thee: for whither thou goest, I will go; and where thou lodgest, I will lodge: thy people shall be my people, and thy God my God.**
>
> **Ruth 1:16**

Ruth's heart was knitted to Naomi; nothing or no one could separate them. Because of Ruth's loyalty and love for Naomi, she was later blessed in her union to Boaz. If you remain faithful to God, He will bless you. Ruth took care of Naomi, and God took care of Ruth. She put the needs of Naomi ahead of her own needs. This is the kind of servanthood I spoke about in chapter one. This kind of servanthood is motivated by genuine — not conditional — love. Though Ruth's conditions changed, her love remained the same toward Naomi. In fact, it probably increased.

When Ruth entered Naomi's country she had no pending job opportunities or living arrangements other than what she would partake of as a result of being Naomi's daughter-in-law. Ruth performed the lowliest of tasks such as following the reapers and gathering fragments of grain which fell to the ground. In other words, she took what she could get for the time being. Many of us would not be happy starting from the bottom. We want God to bless us with things that we haven't worked for. We want "easy blessings."

Ruth gathered grain in the hot sun all day so that she could bring something home at the end of the day for

Naomi. I would imagine that Naomi had to be a good mother-in-law to Ruth in order for Ruth to have such love for her. She was probably the type of mother-in-law that embraced Ruth unselfishly and unjudgingly.

Ruth was a hard worker. She didn't sit around waiting to be pitied. She sought out work and a means to survive. She was focused and patient. She also exhibited contentment until God blessed her. She worked steadily until God blessed her with Boaz (Ruth 4:10,13). This is a valuable lesson to women everywhere that if we delight ourselves in serving God, He will grant us the desires of our heart (Psalm 37:4).

Ruth's love and faithfulness to Naomi caused her to receive love and respect from a people who were not her own blood. She knew how to receive love (or be loved) because she knew how to show love to others. This caused God to pour down His blessings upon her. Ruth later bore Obed who was the father of Jesse, the father of David. (Ruth 4:13,17).

What I like about Ruth is that her love for Naomi was constant. Knowing human nature, I'm sure there were probably times when Ruth's love toward Naomi could have diminished. You see, we tend to be "circumstantial" people. If things are in our favor as it relates to others then we feel happy and secure, but when faced with adversity and those who usually would be in agreement with us are no longer in agreement, then our concern about — and care for — them diminishes. In addition, not many of us would be willing to become acclimated to a place, a people, or ways to which we are not accustomed.

Esther: The Woman Who Exhibited Courage

Courage: "The quality of mind that enables one to face danger with confidence, resolution, and firm control of oneself; bravery."[4]

Esther (formerly known as Hadassah) was an orphan Jewess who lived outside Palestine. She and her family were carried into captivity during the Jews' captivity by

Nebuchadnezzar in 586 B.C. (Esther 2:5-7). Esther was raised by her cousin Mordecai, a Benjamite official, who served as her guardian.

Esther was devoted to her people, the Jews. Esther's courage became the dominating factor in the deliverance of her people. She was a beautiful woman (Esther 2:7). Because of her beauty and God's providence she was chosen to succeed queen Vashti and rose to the status of queen, possessing both power and wisdom.

Esther found herself in the palace of the Persian Empire during the time of Xerxes (or Ahasuerus) who ruled over 127 provinces stretching from India to Cush. For a description of the palace read Esther 1:4-6. When King Ahasuerus took Queen Vashti down from her royal position because she disobeyed him before the princes, God opened an opportunity — through Mordecai — for Esther to rise to the occasion.

King Ahasuerus posted notices requesting that all the beautiful young virgins be brought to the king's harem in Shushan, and noted that the maiden who pleased him would take the place of Queen Vashti. So Mordecai sent forth his lovely cousin Esther.

When Esther was presented to the king, he loved her more than all the other maidens who were gathered. So he sat the royal crown upon her head, and she sat upon the throne of Persia as queen. Although it may have seemed to others that Esther was chosen to be queen primarily because of her beauty, God had a purpose for her that far exceeded her beauty. God permitted Esther to be promoted to this position because He knew what would befall the Jews in days ahead. God is all-knowing!

Esther found herself in proximity to one who hated the Jews and wanted them all dead. This was none other than wicked Haman. He plotted to kill the Jews. He was King Ahasuerus' favorite, his confidant, and was elevated above the other nobles and officials. He demanded that the Jews bow down to him but Mordecai would not. This caused hatred to stir in the heart of Haman toward Mordecai and the Jews. Remember, evil proceeds from the heart. Haman hated the Jews so much that he was intent on destroying this God-fearing people. His hatred, however, did not stop Esther from fighting for the deliverance of her people. She found out about Haman's hatred and feud with Mordecai from her maids and eunuchs. It was enough to distress her but not enough to discourage her.

Esther could have thought about how good life was for her and forget about her people, but she didn't. She could not abandon her people now. That's how God is to His people. He is right beside us in our worst circumstance. Previously, Esther had not revealed her nationality to King Ahasuerus because she was charged not to do so by Mordecai (Esther 2:10). But later on, Esther put her own life on the line by revealing her nationality to King Ahasuerus.

Now Mordecai sent word to Esther by Hatach, asking for help, making her aware that God had placed her in that position for the purpose of delivering her people. The laws of Persia confined the king's wives and thus; it was not possible for Mordecai to have a conference with Esther. These are the words that Mordecai spoke to Esther by Hatach in Esther 4:13,14 (NIV):

When Esther's words were reported to Mordecai, he sent back this answer.

...**"Do not think that because you are in the king's house you alone of all the Jews will escape.**

For if you remain silent at this time, relief and deliverance for the Jews will arise from another place, but you and your father's family will perish. And who knows but that you have come to royal position for such a time as this?"

Woman of God, think about what stage of life you are in as it relates to spiritual things. Has God set you apart for a specific work? Could it be that you are in a specific place and position "for such a time as this?" If so, this place or position may not be a place of comfort. It may be very challenging for you, or you may experience a lot of resistance from others, but if God placed you there, recognize it and make full use of your resources. Listen to the voice of God, and don't complain about where He has placed you or what He is asking you to do. You will miss your blessing as the children of Israel did because of their murmuring, complaining, and rebellion (Numbers 14:1-12, 20-23; 20:23,24).

Esther's first move was a spiritual one. She sent out word that all Jews in Shushan hold a fast in her behalf, and she, too, fasted (Esther 4:16). It is a wise woman who recognizes that she cannot move forward alone but that she needs the prayers and support of those who love her and are like-minded.

Esther then prepared, after seeking God, to go before the king, and her husband, on behalf of her people. Esther was fully aware that it was against the king's law to stand before him except he first summoned her. This was very clear in the words she spoke in chapter four, verse sixteen, "...I will go to the king, even though it is against the law. And if I perish, I perish" (NIV). Esther was willing to give her life in an attempt to save her people.

When Esther finally went before the king the first time, he asked her, "What is it queen Esther? What is your request? Even up to half the kingdom, it will be given you" (Esther 5:3 NIV).

Esther was prudent (cautious, discreet, and sensible). She didn't present everything to the king all at once. She staged it first. She simply informed him that she wanted to host a special banquet and requested his presence along with Haman at this banquet. So the invitation was sent out by the king, at the request of Esther, that Haman join them for dinner. When Haman received the invitation, he became joyful and boasted to his wife and friends that he was invited by the queen to dinner. Haman thought he found favor with Queen Esther. Of course, Haman's wife and friends encouraged him to use this opportunity to protest against Mordecai. Be careful not to try to discredit one's reputation even if you think you have the right to and even if that person has treated you wrongfully. Vengeance belongs to God!

In order to capture Esther's role in the deliverance of the Jews, we must take a brief look at Haman's evil plot against the Jews; therefore allowing us to see how God used Esther to bring deliverance. At the end of dinner — a scrumptious one I'm sure — the king could not sleep so he called for the book of chronicles (or events) to be read to him. He was reminded of the time that Mordecai saved his life from his own two servants who plotted to assassinate him and was made aware that Mordecai had not been rewarded for this deed (Esther 6:1-3). It was at this time that the king heard noise on the outer court of the palace. When he inquired who it was, he was told it was Haman. Haman's visit was to speak to the king about hanging Mordecai on the gallows he was erecting for him. Haman was a real pompous kind of guy. The king's mind, however, was still on rewarding Mordecai for saving his life. So the first thing he asked Haman was, "What shall be done for the man the king delights to honor?" (See Esther 6:4,5 NIV).

Proud Haman thought the king was referring to him so he responded,

..."For the man the king delights to honor,

have them bring a royal robe the king has worn and a horse the king has ridden, one with a royal crest placed on its head.

Then let the robe and horse be entrusted to one of the king's most noble princes. Let them robe the man the king delights to honor, and lead him on the horse through the city streets, proclaiming before him, 'This is what is done for the man the king delights to honor!'"

Esther 6:7-9 (NIV)

What a setup! This is a valuable lesson to us that we should never think more highly of ourselves than we ought (Romans 12:3). God must do the exalting. That way we won't have to worry about being brought down by others or worse yet, by God! Others may attempt to bring you down, but if God set you up, no one can bring you down. As the story goes on, we find that Haman had to do to Mordecai exactly as he suggested to the king in verse six. After all, Mordecai was the man the king delighted to honor.

Now the wise Queen Esther hosted a second banquet in which the king and Haman were invited. Again the king asked Esther:

"...what is your petition? It will be given you. What is your request? Even up to half the kingdom, it will be granted."

Esther 7:2 (NIV)

It is at this time that Esther reveals her nationality to the king and makes her request known to him. Her petition was that the king grant her life; her request was that he spare her people (verse 3). She went on to tell the king how her people had been sold for destruction and slaughter and annihilation. When the king asked Esther, "Who is he? Where is the man who has dared to do such a thing?", Esther answered, "The adversary and enemy is this vile Haman" (Esther 7:4-6 NIV).

Needless to say, Haman was hanged on the very gallows — which was seventy-five feet high — that he had prepared for Mordecai. Not only did God use Esther to save the Jews, but she was given charge over the House of Haman by the king. She in turn showed her loyalty and devotion to her cousin Mordecai by appointing him over Haman's estate. The king's decrees could not be reversed, so additional decrees allowing the Jews to defend themselves were issued. Then, many of the people of the land became Jews, because they were afraid of them (Esther 8:8,11,17 NIV).

Esther was a woman who exhibited courage!

God can use any of us to help bring deliverance in the lives of others just as He used Esther. We are encouraged in the Word of God to acknowledge God in all of our ways and He will lead us (Proverbs 3:6). Make yourself available for God to use; seek His direction and pray on behalf of others, and God will bring deliverance.

Mary: The Favored One

Favor: "Friendly regard shown by a superior. A state of being held in such regard."[5]

Mary who eventually became the mother of Jesus, lived in Nazareth. She later became the wife of Joseph. Mary was a virgin and chaste. I believe God wants His bride — the Church — to be chaste in this day and age; a bride who will not be defiled by other gods, false religions, or ungodly practices. He wants His bride to be free from sin and pure, awaiting His return. God also wants His bride to be known to the world — not ashamed of the Gospel of Jesus Christ. He wants us to stand up for His Word and for what is right.

Mary's life was not prestigious or glamorous. She was not wealthy. If I was to place her in a category, I would probably classify her as "lower class" in terms of earthly and monetary possessions and status. She didn't have much. Even when she gave birth to baby Jesus it was in the lowliest place — a stable. Mary received no praise from others. In other words, she was not recognized, and she was not a part of the "in-crowd." Yet God chose to impregnate her with the Holy Ghost to bring forth the Savior of the world. In fact, when the angel Gabriel came to her announcing that she was blessed among women and highly favored, she thought it strange to receive such a salutation because she considered herself of no importance.

Mary's fame and notability came through the Virgin Birth of Jesus. This event made her unique. It set her apart from all other women regardless of their wealth or status in society. Let's take a look at the birth of Jesus as recorded in Matthew 1:18-23, from Joseph's point of view.

Now the birth of Jesus Christ was on this wise: When as his mother Mary was espoused to Joseph, before they came together, she was found with child of the Holy Ghost.

Then Joseph her husband, being a just man, and not willing to make her a public example, was minded to put her away privily. [Joseph did not want Mary to be treated as a prostitute, or be exposed to public disgrace, especially since they were only contracted to be married, but were not married, and yet Mary was pregnant.]

But while he thought on these things, behold, the angel of the Lord appeared unto him in a dream, saying, Joseph, thou son of David, fear not to take unto thee Mary thy wife: for that which is conceived in her is of the Holy Ghost.

And she shall bring forth a son, and thou shalt call his name JESUS: for he shall save his people from their sins.

Now all this was done, that it might be fulfilled which was spoken of the Lord by the prophet, saying.

Behold, a virgin shall be with child, and shall bring forth a son, and they shall call his name Emmanuel, which being interpreted is, God with us.

From the account of Luke 1:26-35 when the angel appeared to Mary.

And in the sixth month the angel Gabriel was sent from God unto a city of Galilee, named Nazareth.

To a virgin espoused to a man whose name was Joseph, of the house of David; and the virgin's name was Mary.

And the angel came in unto her, and said, Hail, thou that art highly favoured, the Lord is with thee: blessed art thou among women.

And when she saw him, she was troubled at his saying, and cast in her mind what manner of salutation this should be.

And the angel said unto her, Fear not, Mary: for thou hast found favour with God.

And, behold, thou shalt conceive in thy womb, and bring forth a son, and shalt call his name JESUS.

He shall be great, and shall be called the Son of the Highest: and the Lord God shall give unto him the throne of his father David.

And he shall reign over the house of Jacob for ever; and of his kingdom there shall be no end.

Then said Mary unto the angel, How shall this be, seeing I know not a man?

And the angel answered and said unto her, The Holy Ghost shall come upon thee, and the power of the Highest shall overshadow thee: therefore also that holy thing which shall be born of thee shall be called the Son of God.

The story of Mary says a lot to me. Firstly, *God uses ordinary people.* He does this so that no one — including the person being used — can take the credit for that individual's accomplishments, but God. Secondly, God is looking for those who will not allow themselves to be controlled, governed, or defiled with things of this world. He is looking for women who are pure and chaste in thought. Thirdly, God can move in one's life in a quiet, yet powerful way. The birth of Jesus took place in Bethlehem in Judea — in a stable, a place where animals were kept. His birth occurred in the most humble of circumstances yet it was the greatest event in all history.

Although Mary was not well-known, she was highly favored in the sight of God. This is yet another lesson to each of us that although others may not notice us, God sees our abilities and has great plans for our lives. Those of you who already recognize that God is doing great things in your life, remember, *it's not for you to publicize it.* Let God bring it to light. Don't take it upon yourself to announce what God is doing in your life. Just be still and know that He is God. He will pick the time, place, and people with whom to share His great works in your life.

Sarah: The Woman
Who Waited on the Promise

Wait — "To be prepared or ready. A period of time spent in waiting."[6]

Sarah, wife of Abraham was a beautiful young woman. In fact, the Bible says that she was "a fair woman to look upon." Her name was originally Sarai, but God changed her name to Sarah because she would soon become "a mother of nations" through the birth of Isaac, the promised seed (Genesis 17:15,16). Not only was Sarah Abraham's wife, but she was his half-sister on the side of their father Terah. Being married to a close relative was permitted in her day.

Sarah had one problem: She could not conceive children. Many of the women in the Bible were barren, especially the Old Testament women. Although Sarah was beautiful, her beauty could not fill the gap in her life of not being able to have children. Her beauty could not give her the one thing she desired most, which was to conceive and bear a son to Abraham. Yet in spite of this deficiency in her life, Sarah didn't sit around moping. She walked by faith with Abraham. As God spoke to Abraham to get out of his country Ur and go to a land that He would direct him, Sarah obediently followed (Genesis 12:1,2).

I have no doubts that Sarah was a loving, loyal, and devoted wife. In every stage of her life and in every journey she and Abraham took, she was ever learning of God's promises, His covenant, and His ability to provide her needs. She was willing to move forward not knowing exactly what God had in store for her. She remained obedient and faithful to her God. This was the key to Sarah obtaining God's promise, obedience, and faithfulness.

Sarah was truly a "help meet" to Abraham. I believe that she submitted herself to Abraham with confidence that he was in the will of God. In addition, I also believe that Sarah understood what it meant to be in covenant with someone. In fact, she was already in a covenant relationship

43

(her marriage to Abraham); therefore, she had to understand the "covenant" which God made with her and Abraham. Such a covenant would require that she fortify herself especially in a time when it was not certain exactly where God was leading them.

I am convinced that more Christian women need to be strong and supportive of their spouses especially when God is leading them into areas that may not seem clear at first. This is not the time for us to nag and complain. This is the time for us to build up our spouses through prayer and ask God for clear direction on their behalf. Women need to always remember and understand that whatever affects their spouse will affect them, be it positive or negative. This is why I say that we need to pray on behalf of the direction that God is leading our spouses. Never mind just sitting and looking to see what comes next. Be an active part of your husband's destiny by allowing God to use you as an instrument in his life!

We need to encourage and support our spouses in whatever *God* is leading them to do. This may not be easy to do, because many of us don't want to submit to God when He calls us into "unfamiliar territory," much less support our spouses when we don't understand what they are doing or where they are taking us. But be assured that God knows best. We may not see how things will come together, but trust in God. We may fear the process and the unknown but God knows the outcome!

Imagine the obstacles Sarah faced as she journeyed through unfamiliar territory. She and Abraham journeyed through strange and perilous country, not knowing what they would be faced with. As they journeyed, Sarah was often faced with temptations. Even kings desired her because of her beauty (See Genesis 12:10-20).

Sarah had to come out of her comfort zone, that place which was familiar and comfortable to her. She had to come out of her "safe haven." She had to leave the place and people that she was so well acquainted with. She had to leave that stationary lifestyle and routine that satisfied her. Sarah was able to abandon her familiar surroundings because she knew God had something better in store for her and Abraham.

It must have been difficult for her at times though to be constantly moving, never settling down, being a nomad, never taking roots anywhere, un-established. Many of us would not be happy under these circumstances. At the time of Sarah's journeys, she was already 65 and Abraham was 75. Today, when one reaches this age bracket he or she begins to think about — if not prepare for — death. But Sarah's life was just beginning. She believed that God had something great in store for her. This hope is what kept her holding on. She and Abraham and their entourage journeyed along as God directed them.

Abraham and Sarah were not poor. In fact, they were very prosperous. They had menservants and maidservants, sheep, oxen, asses, and other herds and flocks. When his nephew Lot's herdsmen and Abraham's herdsmen got into a conflict, Abraham told Lot to separate himself and his possessions because they both had too much earthly possessions to share the same territory.

Sarah and Abraham had a great entourage but she constantly looked to God her provider, the one who would fulfill His promise to her. God's purpose for Sarah was greater than earthly riches and treasures, and certainly money could not buy what God had promised her.

Women of God, we too must understand that God's purpose for us on this earth is spiritual. If we seek God and His righteousness, everything we need to make it in this life will be given to us (Matthew 6:33). God's purpose for Sarah was a spiritual one, one that would continue for generations to come. Kings of people would come out of her.

Sarah had to be confident concerning the management of the affairs of her household. She took charge of the affairs of her home in the absence of her husband. She had authority and was *respected* as the woman of the house. I believe this was so because Abraham set the example for those in his household to honor Sarah and treat her with respect. I also believe that Abraham led by example. I'm sure he handled Sarah in a certain way so there was no way anyone else would treat her otherwise. He loved her just as he loved himself. In chapter one I talked about the virtuous woman guiding the affairs of her home with grace and dignity. Well, this is what Sarah did.

Sarah had everything going for her except the ability to conceive and bear children. She wanted badly to give her husband a son, one who would carry on the family name. But she recognized that, for whatever reason, God had closed her womb. Sometimes we don't know or understand why we end up in the predicament that we're in. But if we walk upright before God and wait on Him, His purpose for us will unfold *in due time.*

We know that Sarah became discouraged in regards to her barrenness and, I'm sure, assumed that her situation was irreversible and would not change so she sent Abraham in to her handmaiden Hagar that she might bear him a son. "so she said to Abram, The Lord has kept me from having children. Go sleep with my maidservant; perhaps I can build a family through her..." (Genesis 16:2 NIV). God really doesn't need our help! Not in this way. He wants us to have faith in Him and be obedient and patient. Sarah tried to make her situation better by placing Hagar in a position she was never meant to be in.

Sometimes it becomes very difficult to "wait for the promise" but Habakkuk encourages us to wait. "For the vision is yet for an appointed time, but at the end it shall speak, and not lie: though it tarry, wait for it; because it will surely come, it will not tarry" (Habakkuk 2:3). In other words, if God said it, believe it, and wait for that thing that He has shown you to come to pass.

Sarah learned the hard way that the child by Hagar (Ishmael) the Egyptian bond woman was not the child God promised her. It is easier to wait for God's promise to come to fruition than to try to make things happen by our own means, things that in the long run are irreversible.

One day as Abraham was sitting in the doorway of his tent, God sent three men (angels) to visit him. These men were divine messengers sent by God to let Abraham know that his wife would give birth to a son. Sarah, being close by, overheard the conversation between Abraham and the three men. She laughed within herself at the thought of conceiving a child in her old age (Genesis 18:12).

Has God ever given you a promise that sounded ridiculous and impossible? He often does, but remember, He is all powerful and can work against nature on behalf of His people. God would certainly perform a miracle within Sarah, seeing it was not humanly possible, at her age, to have a child. Sarah's childbearing age was long gone. She had already gone through menopause. Let's pause for a brief moment and take a look at menopause and its effect on women. After all, if we live to see the menopausal years before the rapture of the church, we will all experience menopause in one way or another.

Menopause: A Thing of the Past, Present, and Future

This section on menopause is attributed to the work of Jean Lush with Patricia H. Rushford in their book, *Emotional Phases of a Woman's Life*. They describe menopause as the "...final transition between youth and maturity."[7] It is the time during which the complete cessation of the menstrual cycle occurs, or if you will, a time when the woman becomes sterile. Some refer to menopause as "the season of change" or "change of life."

Menopause usually occurs between the ages of 40 and 60 and even into the 60's. The average age, though, is 52. Menopause signals the end of childbearing years, not the end of life. It is like entering a new stage of life with new and exciting opportunities as well as challenges. Life continues after menopause.

Some of the physical symptoms of menopause are erratic menstrual cycles. The word erratic means "not consistent or uniform; irregular."[8] So during the onset of menopause, a woman could see significant changes in her cycle on a monthly basis. The symptom that occurs during menopause that most women are familiar with is "hot flashes" which consists of burning sensations, skin that appears to be flushed, heart palpitations, and anxiety attacks. Some other changes that occur in the body are insomnia, bladder changes, dry skin, breast changes, dizziness, weight gain, bloating, calcium deficiency, etc.

Some women become insecure and lack confidence during menopause because they have entered a stage of life that is new to them. Many women don't fully know what to expect, so it becomes a fear of the unknown. How many of us women have faced something new in life (be it good or bad) and not know how things would play out? This creates a certain amount of anxiety and fear.

As some women reach their menopausal years, because they don't fully understand that it is not the end of their lives, they begin to revert and do things that much younger women would do including how they dress. They do this to try and recapture the years of their youth. It's an act of fear. Fear of what? Menopause not only signals the end of childbearing years, it also signals that a woman is growing older. Perhaps, even to face the rest of her life alone. During this time, women also fear that they will lose their attractiveness and sexuality. No matter what stage of life we are passing through, God still wants us to have self-worth and confidence. Our lives may change, but God never changes. Only He can help us to adapt or handle the challenges that we face as women.

People don't usually fear what they know; they fear what they don't know or understand. One of the best ways to deal with this type of fear is to educate yourself about that which you fear. During the menopausal years, some women end up looking outside of the sanctity of their marriage relationship to find more youthful men who they think can make them feel youthful again. The fact is, no matter what we do to prevent aging, or prevent feeling like we're aging, it will affect all of us. This is all the more reason to serve God diligently in your youth and not let precious years go by. We should remember God in the days of our youth (Ecclesiastes 12:1).

Menopause can be a very emotional experience for women. As the hormone levels fluctuate, so do the emotions. Of course symptoms and emotions vary from woman to woman. Some of the emotional changes women experience during this time are fear of growing older, irritability, depression, mood swings, need for constant reassurance, suspicion, paranoia, sleep disorders, forgetfulness, and loneliness to name a few. As bad as this all sounds, not all women experience these emotional changes, and most women experience very few of them.

By no means have I included this section on menopause because I think it presents unconquerable challenges to women. Instead, I know that God is bigger and greater than anything we face, and He has all things in control. I don't believe the Spirit-filled Christian woman need to be threatened by any of these facts about menopause. Nor do I believe that she will have dreaded, out-of-control experiences. Our fate is in the hands of God, and He looks after His own!

Why did I present this information? I presented it to give you a more vivid, real picture of what Sarah possibly faced and experienced as an older woman. Yet God covenanted with her and Abraham that He would give her a son in her old age. Sarah's situation wasn't too hard for God and neither is yours! Never let your present circumstances determine your future. We serve a God of possibilities. "For with God nothing shall be impossible" (Luke 1:37).

Because God is a God of possibilities, He made Sarah's womb "alive" and performed a miracle that would not only fulfill but also seal His covenant with Abraham (Romans 4:19). God would not only perform the miracle of conception, but He would cause Sarah's body to reproduce as if it were 70 years younger, considering that she was ninety-nine years old when she had Isaac (Genesis 21).

So God kept His promise and Isaac was born (Genesis 21:1-7). Sarah nurtured Isaac, and even in her old age, had the privilege of indulging in motherhood for about 28 years after the birth of Isaac. As Isaac got older, Abraham's faith would be tested in the offering of Isaac as a burnt offering. It often seems that God allows us to be tested in the areas of our blessings, the area of promise that He has given to us. It's not strange that oftentimes the things God has blessed us with He, in turn, expects us to bless others with. One can only imagine how Abraham felt after having waited for years for the son of the promise to have to exhibit faith and obedience toward God's instruction to offer Isaac as a burnt offering. Let's take a look at the biblical account of this story.

> Some time later God tested Abraham. He said to him, "Abraham!" "Here I am," he replied.

> Then God said, "Take your son, your only son, Isaac, whom you love, and go to the region of Moriah. Sacrifice him there as a burnt offering on one of the mountains I will tell you about."

> Early the next morning Abraham got up and saddled his donkey. He took with him two of his servants and his son Isaac. When he had cut enough wood for the burnt offering, he set out for the place God had told him about.

> On the third day Abraham looked up and saw the place in the distance. He said to his servants, "Stay here with the donkey while I and the boy go over there. We will worship and then we will come back to you."

> Abraham took the wood for the burnt offering and placed it on his son Isaac, and he himself carried the fire and the knife. As the two of them went on together,

> Isaac spoke up and said to his father Abraham, "Father?" "Yes, my son?" Abraham replied.

> "The fire and the wood are here," Isaac said, "but where is the lamb for the burnt offering?"

Abraham answered, "God himself will provide the lamb for the burnt offering, my son." And the two of them went on together.

When they reached the place God had told him about, Abraham built an altar there and arranged the wood on it. He bound his son Isaac and laid him on the altar, on top of the wood.

Then he reached out his hand and took the knife to slay his son.

But the angel of the Lord called out to him from heaven, 'Abraham! Abraham!' 'Here I am,' he replied.

"Do not lay a hand on the boy," he said. "Do not do anything to him. Now I know that you fear God, because you have not withheld from me your son, your only son."

Abraham looked up and there in a thicket he saw a ram caught by its horns. He went over and took the ram and sacrificed it as a burnt offering instead of his son.

Genesis 22:1-13 (NIV)

I am not inclined to believe that Sarah knew anything about the sacrificing of Isaac. I believe that God dealt exclusively with Abraham in regard to the sacrificing of Isaac because perhaps, Sarah would not have been able to handle receiving such a blessing by God only to sacrifice that blessing back to God. Isn't it ironic that God would ask one to give up the very thing (or person) that He gave to that individual as a blessing? Yet we know that Abraham's situation as it related to the sacrificing of Isaac was a test of his faith in God and obedience toward Him.

Through the birth of Isaac, the promised seed, Sarah became one of the most well-known, well-respected women in the Bible. She truly was a woman who learned how to wait on God.

Just like Sarah and Abraham, many of us will be — if not already — tested in the area(s) that we feel secure and confident in — those things that we consider a blessing. But if we put our complete trust in God and obey His

Word, realizing that God knows what is best for us, then all things will work together for our good (Romans 8:28).

Jochebed: A Woman of Faith

Faith: "Confident belief; trust. Belief in God."[9]

Jochebed was born in Egypt. She was a descendant of Levi and the wife of Amram who was of the house of Levi (Numbers 26:59, Exodus 2:1). She was the mother of Miriam, Aaron, and Moses, the great lawgiver.

I can't help but think that there were some values instilled in Jochebed concerning the "traditions" of the priestly line, being that she was a part of that line. After all, her husband Amram was the grandson of Levi. Although the priestly line — in terms of traditions and duties — may not have been set in place until after the departure of the children of Israel out of Egypt, I believe that those who were a part of this line prior to Israel's departure out of Egypt held on to certain priestly traditions and practices within their family circle (See Exodus 28). No doubt Jochebed too, became familiar with those traditions and raised her children to know, understand, respect, and practice those traditions. In fact, we know that her son Aaron was set apart to be a priest. (See Exodus 6:20, Numbers 8:5-14; 18:1-7, and 26:57-65).

I believe Jochebed exercised discernment in her household as it pertained to the things of God for her family. This was evident at the time of Moses' birth (Exodus 2:1,2).

During this time, a decree was issued throughout Egypt by Pharaoh to kill all Hebrew male babies at birth because there were too many of them already (Exodus 1:15-17). The king of Egypt feared that the Israelites would join the enemies of the Egyptians if war broke out, and that they (the Israelites and "the enemy") would fight against the Egyptians to destroy them.

Jochebed, being a godly woman, not only loved her child, but also believed that God had a purpose for Moses and that Moses would have a destiny in life. She wanted her child to live. Jochebed saw that Moses was a good child, and she exercised her faith in God on Moses' behalf.

> **But when she could hide him no longer,** [after three months] **she got a papyrus basket for him and coated it with tar and pitch. Then she placed the child in it and put it among the reeds along the bank of the Nile.**
>
> **Exodus 2:3 (NIV)**

During this time Jochebed must have prayed and believed that God would allow some descent, compassionate person to find the basket with baby Moses in it. It was in fact Pharaoh's daughter that found the basket, but it was Jochebed who was privileged to nurse her own son upon being hired by Pharaoh's daughter (Exodus 2:5-13). This is what we call God's divine providence.

We later find that Moses became the Hebrew lawgiver. He imparted the Ten Commandments and other laws, ordinances, and precepts to the children of Israel as God gave them to him. He was a great leader whom God raised up to deliver Israel from under the oppression of the Egyptians. Had Jochebed given up at the decree of Pharaoh, and not exercised faith in God, perhaps she would have never experienced the self-gratification and joy of knowing that her son would become one of the greatest leaders of Israel.

Women of God, no matter what the situation seems like, and no matter who has issued a decree against you and your godly efforts, stand strong and have faith in God (Mark 11:22). But remember, faith without works is dead (James 2:17). Allow your faith to move you to action as God leads you. Don't allow anyone to take from you the thing that God has allowed you to birth spiritually. It is your "baby" so to speak. You fight for it! You have a responsibility to nurture whatever God puts in your hands whether they are gifts, talents, abilities, or ministries. Listen for the voice of God in your life and He will instruct you exactly what to do in any given situation.

Jochebed certainly was one of the great mothers of the Bible. She was a woman of faith. She displayed active faith in God.

Just as there were virtuous women in biblical days, there are virtuous women in the body of Christ today. I hope that this chapter provided you with some insightful things about the strength and character of women throughout history, especially women of God.

Women, you are important in the kingdom of God. Seek God and find out what your purpose is in life. Allow yourself to be used by God, and pray to God for strength for the tasks that lie ahead.

[1] *The American Heritage Dictionary*, p. 539.

[2] *The American Heritage Dictionary*, p. 362.

[3] *The American Heritage Dictionary*, p. 405.

[4] *The American Heritage Dictionary*, p. 161.

[5] *The American Heritage Dictionary*, p. 257.

[6] *The American Heritage Dictionary*, p. 764.

[7] Jean Lush with Patricia H. Rushford, *Emotional Phases of a Woman's Life* (Michigan: Fleming H. Revell Publishers a division of Baker Book House Company, 1994), p. 175.

[8] *The American Heritage Dictionary*, p. 240.

[9] *The American Heritage Dictionary*, p. 253.

Chapter 3
A Message to the
"Seasoned" Christian Woman

I want to say to the older, "seasoned" women who have served God faithfully over the years, "The younger women need your wisdom." Don't think that because you are older now that it is time to move out of the way and let the young women do their thing. In a sense, yes, the young women need space to mature and grow in God as well as to take on the tasks that God has put before them, but you are still needed. There is a place within the body of Christ that only you can fill. You have been through things that some of the younger women have not yet faced, and they need you to share your experiences and wisdom with them.

On the other hand, over the years, I've heard *some* older women say, "The older women are supposed to teach the younger women" (Titus 2:3,4). All too often this statement is made in the "spirit of pride" which God hates. Sadly enough, the women that I've heard make this statement are sitting still doing nothing. There is no need to be non-supportive of the work that *God* has placed in the hands of younger women. As an older, seasoned woman, experience allows God to use you to help them.

We are living in a day and age when younger women are moving forward in spite of obstacles and criticisms. Young women today are determined, motivated, and aggressive about God's business. What older women need to understand, is that young women need their support more than they need *destructive* criticisms! One who constantly complains about the manner in which things are done but is not willing to participate or be used — when given the opportunity — to make things better, should not complain!! This may sound harsh, but it's reality.

Young women *will* respect the older women as they offer *constructive* criticism. What am I saying? How you approach someone will determine the response you get from the person, be it positive or negative. Constructive criticism is not a negative thing. Oh no, it's positive. It allows one to show another his or her "shortcomings" (not necessarily pertaining to sin), or show one how to do a better job at what he or she is doing. Constructive criticism should be done in love. This kind of criticism is not harsh, selfish, or impatient but is rather the voice of meekness and patience. It will cause one to strive for nothing less than excellence. This is the kind of support the young women need today.

Just look back into your life as a saved woman, at the things God used to do through you. Look at how you used to minister to those in the body of Christ. What are you doing now? You ran well but who can you blame now for your stagnation? (Galatians 5:7,8).

You may feel that you have done your share over the years, but there is still more for you to do — be an example to the young women! You do have a responsibility to "teach the younger women." So when you see the younger women trying their best to establish works for God, support them. By the same token, when you see them struggling with challenges in their lives, don't sit back and talk about them if you have contributed nothing to their growth, and especially if you've had some of these same challenges in your youth or perhaps *now.*

The young women need strong mentors that they can look up to just like the ones profiled in chapter two. Remember, only what you do for Christ will last. Having knowledge and wisdom is no good if you don't share it with others. What God has invested in you is for the edifying and perfecting of the saints. That is, all saints. The gifts that God has placed in you are worth so much that they cannot be purchased. Share your gifts and abilities with the young women as God directs you. Even more so, share your advice and wisdom.

I cannot close this chapter without including a message to the younger women since they are referenced throughout this chapter. I encourage the young women to respect the older women in the church (and outside the church) like the respect Ruth had for Naomi. You don't have to agree with everything or see "eye to eye," but you must respect the older women, just as they must show respect toward you.

Value and embrace the wisdom of the older women. In fact, seek after it. Get to know some of the older women in your local church, and ask them to share their knowledge and wisdom with you. You will be surprised to know the things that they can relate to because of their experiences. Many of us can learn from their experiences in a very positive way. Do not isolate yourself from the older women, make them a part of your life. Who said that you only have to be around women of your age? Let's break tradition — or what is normally done, and branch out to the older women. If God spares your life, you too will one day be termed an "older woman." The older women can give you guidance in a lot of areas as God leads you to share your concerns and ideas with them.

Chapter 4

Obstacles and Hindrances That Prevent a Forward Move in God

I have devoted this chapter to addressing some of the areas of difficulties we face as women, because, in order to exhibit virtuous characteristics (or qualities) and be used by God, we must be healed in our emotions, our mind, and our desires.

In this chapter, I present, address, and provide scriptural advice for these areas of difficulties within one's life. I focus on obstacles that prevent women (individually and collectively) from moving forward and accepting the call that God has placed in their lives. It's my desire that women of all denominations, backgrounds, ethnicities, and ages will, after reading this chapter, recognize and confront the obstacles in their own lives. My desire is that women seek to overcome these obstacles, using the Word of God and prayer, and by allowing the unconditional love of God to shine through them toward others. It is important that in every situation, our lives line up with the Word of God. This will take great effort, but it is a reachable goal.

The following are areas that present themselves as obstacles if not brought under subjection to the Spirit of God and His Word. Many women have been affected, destroyed, and have even destroyed others because these areas were out of control in their lives. Let's take a look at some of these obstacles.

Brokenhearted/Broken

Brokenhearted — "Overcome by grief or despair."[1]

Broken — "Shattered: having gaps or breaks: crushed."[2]

Many of us have been broken in one way or another. There are many things that cause one to "break" such as: loss of a loved one, failure in a career or marriage, adverse circumstances, or personal conflicts with family, friends, and those in the church.

We become broken when we feel that we can't stand under pressure, be it emotional, spiritual, or physical. During this time, we become vulnerable to that which we feel we can't overcome. We become broken through our relationships and often feel that in order to be whole again, we must move on to find new friends and seek new relationships — only to find that we can, and in most cases do, become broken even in our *new* relationships. But God "...healeth the broken in heart, and bindeth up their wounds" (Psalm 147:3).

One usually encounters extreme tests and trials that lead to brokenness. It is often these tests and trials that break an individual. One can also become broken from trying again and again to accomplish something that is not within his or her power to accomplish. In cases like this, we need to understand that God can use our brokenness to make us new — even better — all over again. Being broken gives God the opportunity to work things out. Let us look at the story of the potter.

> **So I went down to the potter's house, and I saw him working at the wheel.**
>
> **But the pot he was shaping from the clay was marred in his hands; so the potter formed it into *another* pot, shaping it as seemed best to him.**
>
> **Then the word of the Lord came to me:**

> **"O house of Israel, can I not do with you as this potter
> does?" declares the Lord. "Like the clay in the hand of the
> potter, so are you in my hand, O house of Israel."**
>
> **Jeremiah 18:3-6 (NIV)**

Notice, the potter formed the pot into another pot and
shaped it as it seemed best to him. God does the same
thing. He uses our experiences (the negative ones) to
make something better of us. If the pot wasn't messed up,
there would be no need for the potter to re-shape it.

No matter how bad your situation seems or how broken you feel, God is able to make and shape you all over
again. All hope is not lost! You must acknowledge God as
your Father and realize that you are the work of His hands
(Isaiah 64:8).

We often fail to recognize that being broken gives us
an opportunity to open ourselves up to God, the One who
can and will mend our hearts. It also gives us an opportunity to be healed of all our hurts and pains. This can only
happen when we are honest with ourselves and realize
that *sometimes* we have no control over our situations or
life's circumstances. The important thing to remember is
that God cares for us and can mend our brokenness, no
matter how severe. God is our potter, and He wants to
make us new again in spite of the broken pieces of our
lives.

We become broken when we fail to look to God and
wait on the fulfillment of His purpose for our lives.

We also become broken when we put our trust in
human flesh more than in God, as instructed in His Word.
The Word of God tells us that...

> **It is better to trust in the Lord than to put confidence in
> man.**
>
> **It is better to trust in the Lord than to put confidence in
> princes.**
>
> **Psalm 118:8,9**

Hurt — "To feel or cause to feel physical or emotional pain: to do harm to: offend: hamper."[3]

Now more than ever, women in the body of Christ are hurting. Hurt stems from, and is a result of, being broken. One who is broken and fails to allow Christ to heal him or her will experience greater hurts and pains that will take longer to heal and will spread into many other areas of that person's life.

When Do We Hurt?

We hurt when:
- we have been betrayed and friends and family turn against us.
- trust has been broken.
- we have been let down.
- others don't understand us.
- others don't embrace us.
- others don't accept or receive us.
- no one seems to care for us.
- we are talked about in a negative way.
- we are falsely accused.
- good intentions are misunderstood.
- others pre-judge us.
- others use and misuse us.
- others don't support our efforts.
- others don't believe in us.
- others speak negative words into our lives.
- we feel unloved and unwanted.
- we hurt from past experiences.

Sometimes these experiences are ones that occurred before we even experienced the saving grace of God, yet they can still cause us to hurt after accepting Christ in our lives.

Notice, most — if not all — hurtful experiences occur as a result of wrongful (or interpreted to be wrongful) or offensive words or deeds done by one toward another. One does not usually walk around hurting because of his/her own self. It is usually because of someone else, or something else.

I'm sure that many of you have already identified with some of the hurtful areas I've listed, but remember, you are not alone. Women are experiencing hurt all over the world yet we serve the Master Physician, the One who can make us whole: His name is Jesus.

"This is what the Lord says: 'Your wound is incurable, your injury beyond healing.

"'There is no one to plead your cause, no remedy for your sore, no healing for you.

"'*But I will restore health and heal your wounds, declares the Lord,* **because you are called an outcast, Zion for whom no one cares.'"**
Jeremiah 30:12,13,17 (NIV)

How many times, in reading this passage, have you felt that this was descriptive of you or of how you felt? It is comforting to know that God cares for us no matter what! He wants to bring healing into our lives — if we would just let Him. (See Scriptures on healing: Proverbs 16:24, Luke 9:11, Exodus 15:26, Isaiah 58:8, Jeremiah 33:6).

The act of healing involves restoration. Sometimes in order for a complete healing to take place, one must also be restored or "brought back" to a previous or original condition. The act of restoration definitely demonstrates and reflects God's compassion and mercy toward human beings.

Bitter — "Marked by intensity or severity (as of distress or hatred): extremely harsh or cruel."[4]

When our hurts don't heal, they turn to bitterness toward that person or thing that has caused us to hurt. We must be very careful not to allow bitterness to take root. Bitterness is a progressed stage of hatred. Paul admonishes believers to get rid of *all* bitterness because this grieves the Holy Spirit (Ephesians 4:30-32). Along with bitterness comes unforgiveness. Bitterness can lodge itself so deep within one's spirit (heart) that he/she finds it very difficult, even impossible, to forgive others. This is dangerous.

Since forgiveness is often tied into bitterness, I would like to address it further. First of all, forgiveness is giving up your right to hurt someone else. The moment you begin to forgive, you begin to heal. However, when one is bitter against another, the last thing that person wants to do is forgive, but God can enable one to forgive if he/she truly wants to. One who is unwilling to forgive others will not obtain forgiveness from God. Before we receive forgiveness from God, we must demonstrate the same to one another (Mark 11:25,26).

Why does God put such a demand as forgiveness on us? Because forgiveness demonstrates the love of God from one person to another. It is the love of God that is shed abroad in our hearts that allows us to forgive others.

The disciple John exhorts us to brotherly love in First John 4:20. He asks the question,

If a man say, I love God, and hateth his brother, he is a liar: for he that loveth not his brother whom he hath seen, how can he love God whom he hath not seen?

If we are not careful, we will walk around declaring that we love God and yet hate each other. This is not the "God-kind" of love. I'm sure that you can see how one thing easily leads to another. Bitterness encompasses unforgiveness, and the ability to forgive demonstrates the love of God which must be shown toward others first before one can truly say "I love God."

Allowing bitterness to fester will cripple you spiritually, affecting your progress in God. Oh yes, bitterness and hatred will stop you dead in your tracks! Remember, I stated earlier that bitterness is a progressed stage of hatred. This kind of bitterness will block up your ability to be productive. It will stop the anointing of God from flowing in you.

This is not God's will for you, my sister. In fact, listen to what God has planned for your life.

"For I know the plans I have for you," declares the Lord, "plans to prosper you and not harm you, *plans to give you hope and a future."*
                                                            Jeremiah 29:11 (NIV)

When you get bitterness out of you, the promise will come.

Bitterness will defile you! Let's look at the words of Paul the apostle in Hebrews 12:1,15.

Wherefore seeing we also are compassed about with so great a cloud of witnesses, let us lay aside every weight, and the sin which doth so easily beset us, and let us run with patience the race that is set before us,

Looking diligently lest any man fail of the grace of God; lest any root of bitterness springing up trouble you, and thereby many be defiled.

A "bitter root" refers to a spirit and attitude characterized by intense animosity and resentment.

Resent — "To feel or exhibit annoyance or indignation at."[5]

Bitterness can most definitely be directed toward persons in the church. Bitterness in the body of Christ can spread and defile many. My dear sister, if you are experiencing bitterness, I plead with you today to turn it over to God. Give Him your hurts and let Him heal you so that He can raise you up to minister to others. In your bitterness, pray and pour out your soul to the Lord as Hannah did.

In bitterness of soul Hannah wept much and prayed to the Lord.

..."I am a woman who is deeply troubled...I was pouring out my soul to the Lord."**
                                                            1 Samuel 1:10,15 (NIV)

Envy — "Painful or resentful awareness of another's advantages: an object of envy."[6]

Envy is the beginning stage of jealousy. It causes one to resentfully become aware of another's advantages. Envy will cause you to attempt to imitate the words and actions of the one you are envious of. It is deceptive. It causes one to operate out of an unhealthy desire to be like someone else or to possess the earthly accomplishments, substances, or status of another, in order to be recognized or feel a sense of achievement. Envy is an infiltration and imposition against that which God has intended one to be. Envy often comes as a result of dissatisfaction or lack of contentment in one's life.

James 3:14-16 tells us that where envying and strife is, there is confusion and every evil work, and we know that God is not the author of confusion (See 1 Corinthians 14:33).

Some of the early signs of envy are:

• Feeling threatened by another's accomplishments and status to the degree that you feel you have to be "like" that individual by imitating or copying that person.

• Feeling that you should be the one in a particular position because you deserve it or because you are better qualified.

One thing that we need to understand is that envy will cause us to think that we can justify our attitude and behavior toward others by believing and confessing the following:

"I'm better than he/she is."

"I can do a better job."

"I've been saved longer and have more experience; therefore, I should have gotten the position."

"I'm trained (qualified) and skilled in this area."

To a degree, *some* of the above points may very well be true but how important is it for you to prove this to others? What is your motive, and who will you hurt in the process?

• Envy will cause you to see the other person as the opposer, "the enemy" when in fact he/she is not.

• Envy will cause you to dislike others for no apparent reason at all.

• Envy will cause you to wrongfully judge others without any knowledge or facts of the individual(s) or the situation at hand.

• Envy will cause you to contaminate others with negative information (even lies) about the person or people you are envious of. Envy can have a subtle face! One who is truly overtaken with envy can begin to "infect" or "poison" others without the other person knowing up front what's really going on unless he/she is tapped into God.

These are just some of the early signs of envy taking root in a person. If you feel any of these or have acted upon any, you need to offer true repentance to God (and perhaps the persons involved) and not allow yourself to be controlled by envy any more. It isn't worth it! God has so much He wants to do in your life, and you have so much you can offer others. Why waste your time being eaten up with envy? Women of God, shake yourselves from the grips of envy. Let God arise in you!

I am often amazed how we allow ourselves to become envious or even jealous of others when, if we look deep inside ourselves, we would see that we have so much to offer. The problem is that we become over-concerned with the success of others, and it sometimes blinds us to the abilities, strengths, talents, and gifts that God has placed within us. Just imagine how strong and effective we could be as women of God if we join our forces together, pray for one another, support one another, and rejoice with one another!

I believe in my spirit that every sincere, faithful, committed woman of God will be raised up *in God's appointed time.* So if you feel that you have been faithful serving God and others and know that God has invested something special in you, yet there seems to be no opportunity (or room) for you to operate in that area, just wait — *in due season God will exalt you.*

An important thing to remember is that it doesn't pay to be envious or jealous of anyone because you don't know what one has gone through — or the sacrifices that were made — in order for that person to be used by God. The question to ask yourself is, "Am I willing to endure tests and trials? Am I willing to make the sacrifice that it would take to become what God wants me to be?"

The Word of God calls those "blessed" who persevere under trial. In other words, that person who persists in spite of difficulties will receive the crown of life that God has promised to those who love Him (James 1:12). We go through tests and trials that our faith in God may be proved (1 Peter 1:6,7).

In order to be anointed in service for God, one must be tried or proved. God already declared in His Word, through the mouth of Zechariah, that He will bring His people into the fire.

> **"...I will refine them like silver and test them like gold. They will call on my name and I will answer them; I will say, 'They are my people,' and they will say, 'The Lord is our God.'"**
>
> **Zechariah 13:9 (NIV)**

There is something that fire does that nothing else can do. Fire burns to the point that nothing is left but ashes. Fire burns out imperfections and impurities; it refines. In the case of gold and silver, fire burns to perfection. It gets to the core beauty of these objects. In the spiritual realm, as it pertains to the people of God, fire "burns out the beauty" in us. Notice, I didn't say fire "brings out," it "burns out!" Fire reveals and discloses. The process itself isn't easy, neither is it pleasant but the outcome of the process is what determines whether or not the object has any life-value, endurance, and beauty.

Jealous(y) — "Demanding complete devotion: *suspicious* of a rival or of one believed to enjoy an advantage."[7]

Jealousy is the sister of envy. It is a very real, powerful, and destructive emotion. It will cause one to seek to intentionally hurt another, to seek out the destruction of another. Jealousy comes about as a result of one's own insecurities or inadequacies. It takes root when one feels he/she deserves something or someone more than another person does. When one feels that he/she can do something better than another person to the degree of trying to destroy or bring down that person, then jealousy has taken root.

The Word of God says that "jealousy is as cruel as the grave." Jealousy will cause one to seek to take the life of another spiritually, emotionally, and physically by whatever means necessary! We see it all the time in society.

We see this progressed stage of jealousy when Joseph's brothers plotted to kill him but ended up selling him to the Ishmaelites. Let's take a look at Genesis 37:3,4,12-27 (NIV).

Now Israel loved [favored] Joseph more than any of his other sons, because he had been born to him in his old age; and he made a richly ornamented robe for him.

When his brothers saw that their father loved him more than any of them, they hated him and could not speak a kind word to him.

Now his brothers had gone to graze their father's flocks near Shechem,

and Israel said to Joseph, "As you know, your brothers are grazing the flocks near Shechem. Come, I am going to send you to them." "Very well," he replied.

So he said to him, "Go and see if all is well with your brothers and with the flocks, and bring word back to me." Then he sent him off from the Valley of Hebron. When Joseph arrived at Shechem,

a man found him wandering around in the fields and asked him, "What are you looking for?"

He replied, "I'm looking for my brothers. Can you tell me where they are grazing their flocks?"

"They have moved on from here," the man answered, I heard them say, "Let's go to Dothan." So Joseph went after his brothers and found them near Dothan.

But they saw him in the distance, and before he reached them, they plotted to kill him.

"Here comes that dreamer!" They said to each other.

"Come now, let's kill him and throw him into one of these cisterns and say that a ferocious animal devoured him. *Then we'll see what comes of his dreams.*"

When Reuben heard this, he tried to rescue him from their hands. "Let's not take his life," he said.

"Don't shed any blood. Throw him into this cistern here in the desert, but don't lay hand on him." Reuben said this to rescue him from them and take him back to his father.

So when Joseph came to his brothers, they stripped him of his robe — the richly ornamented robe he was wearing —

and they took him and threw him into the cistern. Now the cistern was empty; there was no water in it.

As they sat down to eat their meal, they looked up and saw a caravan of Ishmaelites coming from Gilead. Their camels were loaded with spices, balm and myrrh, and they were on their way to take them down to Egypt.

Judah said to his brothers, "What will we gain if we kill our brother and cover up his blood?

"Come, let's sell him to the Ishmaelites and not lay our hands on him; after all, he is our brother, our own flesh and blood." His brothers agreed.

So what led to Joseph's brothers being jealous of him? It was the favor (love) that Jacob had for Joseph but in actuality it was his dreams. The kind of "favor" Jacob had for Joseph was a type of grace or graciousness toward Joseph. In other words, Jacob had reason to find favor in Joseph. What was his reason? Joseph was the son of his old age. Therefore, Jacob showed goodwill to Joseph. To be in favor with is to find "grace" with.

It is evident from reading Genesis 37 that Joseph's brothers hated and became jealous of him not only because he was his father's favorite, but also because of his dreams. I'd like to deviate for a moment and take this opportunity to address the subject of "favoritism." Is it wrong; is it right? The Word of God will shed light on the subject.

Let's take a look at James 2:1-5,9,10 (NIV).

My brothers, as believers in our glorious Lord Jesus Christ, don't show favoritism.

Suppose a man comes into your meeting wearing a gold ring and fine clothes, and a poor man in shabby clothes also comes in.

If you show special attention to the man wearing fine clothes and say "Here's a good seat for you," but say to the poor man, "You stand there" or "Sit on the floor by my feet,"

have you not discriminated among yourselves and become judges with evil thoughts?

Listen, my dear brothers. Has not God chosen those who are poor in the eyes of the world to be rich in faith and to inherit the kingdom he promised those who love him?

But if you show favoritism, you sin and are convicted by the law as lawbreakers.

For whoever keeps the whole law and yet stumbles at just one point is guilty of breaking all of it.

The Full Life Study Bible New International Version clearly defines and describes "favoritism" as the following: "To show favoritism is to give special attention to people because of their wealth, clothing, or position." There are several reasons why this is wrong. "(1) It displeases God, who does not look at the outward appearance but at the heart (1 Samuel 16:7). (2) *It is not motivated by genuine love for all* (verse 8). (3) ...instead of...accepting persons on the basis of their faith in Christ, *we unjustly favor people for the advantage we might receive.*"[8] (See also Leviticus 19:15, Jude verse 16).

In God's eyes, everyone is precious. He loves all of humanity; that's why He gave His only begotten Son (Jesus) that those who receive Him would gain eternal life (John 3:16). It is not profitable to build so-called friendships based solely on what others can do for you because when they become unable or unwilling to comply with your wishes or needs, then that relationship will dissolve. Obviously if *true friendship* exists, those involved will experience the benefits of each other's talents, abilities, gifts, and strengths. But liking or accepting people primarily for what they can do or what they possess is wrong and selfish! I believe this is the kind of "favoritism" James speaks about. It is sinful in the eyes of God. The only way we can get rid of the spirit of partiality or "favoritism" is by possessing and exercising godly wisdom (See James 3:17).

Jacob's favoritism, however, toward Joseph was different. Joseph had nothing to give in terms of earthly possessions and he probably could not do anything for his father that his brothers could not also do — perhaps even better — at the time. It was not until God used Joseph's adversities to elevate him in the land of Egypt — knowing the hardship his family would suffer — that he was able to help his family in a way that none of his brothers could. This was by divine purpose, and even then, Joseph remained humble before God.

God took Joseph's adversities brought on by his brothers' jealousy and turned things around for his good and the good of his family and others. His entire family ended up looking to him for their daily provision. I provided this first example about the jealousy of Joseph's brothers simply to show how it can make one act — or things it can make one do — toward another (or others).

Another example of jealousy took place between Saul and David. I will begin by introducing David and the office he held at the time, then give some background information about Saul (based on 1 Samuel 15). In addition I will look at how David was chosen king over Israel as well as some of David's accomplishments, before addressing exactly what it was that caused Saul to become jealous of David.

David the Shepherd Boy

Shepherd — "One who herds, guards, and cares for sheep."[9]

Shepherds feed the sheep just as pastors feed the people of God with the Word of God.

Most of us are familiar with the story of Saul and how he was rejected by God as king over Israel because of his disobedience.

> **Now go, attack the Amalekites and *totally destroy everything* that belongs to them. *Do not spare them;* put to death men and women, children and infants, cattle and sheep, camels and donkeys.**
>
> **Then Saul attacked the Amalekites all the way from Havilah to Shur, to the east of Egypt.**
>
> ***But Saul and the army spared* Agag and the best of the sheep and cattle, the fat calves and lambs — everything that was good. These they were unwilling to destroy completely, but everything that was despised and weak they totally destroyed.**
>
> **Then the word of the Lord came to Samuel:**
>
> **"I am grieved that I have made Saul king...."**
>
> **1 Samuel 15:3,7,9-11 (NIV)**

As believers we learn a valuable lesson from this story. That is, "...To obey is better than sacrifice, and to heed is better than the fat of rams" (1 Samuel 15:22 NIV). If we do *exactly* what God instructs us to do we will be spared a lot of unnecessary grief and heartache. This is easier said than done, but I know this from experience.

Israel was in need of another king to take Saul's place and God sent Samuel to visit Jesse of Bethlehem to anoint one of his sons as king over Israel. Once Jesse was informed of the purpose of Samuel's visit, he allowed his seven sons (Eliab, Abinadab, Shammah, and so on) to pass before Samuel. Jesse was confident that God had selected one of the seven to be king over Israel. However, God had not chosen any of them (1 Samuel 16:6-10). Finally, Samuel inquired of Jesse whether he had any more sons (you see, Samuel was certain that the man who would become the next king over Israel was in that household; otherwise, God would not have sent him there). Jesse told Samuel about his youngest son David who was a shepherd boy and was presently in the field looking after the sheep. Jesse had no intention — before being asked of Samuel — to introduce David to Samuel. Jesse probably figured there was no way that David would be the one because he was too young and just a shepherd boy. It sounds very much like how some believers think today.

This story is a perfect example of how God uses ordinary people. He uses the simple to confound the wise (1 Corinthians 1:27). God had already let Samuel know (as shown in previous verses) that He does not look at the things that man looks at. Man looks at the outward appearance but God looks at the heart.

> **So he went and had him** [David] **brought in. He was ruddy [reddish, rosy in color], with a fine appearance and handsome features. Then the Lord said, "Rise and anoint him; he is the one."**
>
> **So Samuel took the horn of oil and anointed him in the presence of his brothers, and from that day on the Spirit of the Lord came upon David in power....**
>
> **1 Samuel 16:12,13 (NIV)**

The basic meaning of the word "anoint" "is simply to 'smear' something on an object."[10] To anoint also means to consecrate. One who is anointed has been "set apart" for an office or function. This was a common practice in the Old Testament for kings to be anointed for their office.

If God has anointed you to stand in a specific office, His presence should accompany you every time you step into that office!

From the time Samuel anointed David, God began to use him mightily for His glory. *The works that God does through you should always draw attention to, and bring glory to Him.*

In the same way, let your light shine before men, that they may see your good deeds and praise your Father in heaven.
Matthew 5:16 (NIV)

Many of us know that David was also a gifted musician. He played the harp. In fact, he played for Saul on several occasions to drive away the evil spirit that troubled Saul as a result of his disobedience to God. Watch out! You may have unintentionally invited evil spirits into your life by *willfully* disobeying God's instruction to you.

We get in trouble for disobeying God's instruction. Oftentimes we are too busy trying to prove to others *that* which God only intended *for us to know* and understand at the time. If God instructs you to do a specific thing at a specific time, just do it! More than likely, others will not understand anyway because that word is not for them.

We know that David challenged Goliath, the Philistine giant, when no one else would.

A champion named Goliath, who was from Gath, came out of the Philistine camp. He was over nine feet tall.

Goliath stood and shouted to the ranks of Israel, "Why do you come out and line up for battle? Am I not a Philistine, and are you not the servants of Saul? Choose a man and have him come down to me."

For forty days the Philistines came forward every morning and evening and took his stand.

David asked the men standing near him, "What will be done for the man who kills this Philistine and removes this disgrace from Israel? Who is this uncircumcised Philistine that he should defy the armies of the living God?"

Then he [David] took his staff in his hand, chose five smooth stones from the stream, put them in the pouch of his shepherd's bag and, with his sling in his hand, approached the Philistine.

David said to the Philistine, "You come against me with a sword and spear and javelin, but I come against you in the name of the Lord Almighty, the God of the armies of Israel, whom you have defiled."

...David ran quickly toward the battle line to meet him.

Reaching into his bag and taking out a stone, he slung it and struck the Philistine on the forehead. The stone sank into his forehead, and he fell facedown on the ground.

So David triumphed over the Philistine with a sling and a stone; without a sword in his hand he struck down the Philistine and killed him.

David ran and stood over him. He took hold of the Philistine's sword and drew it from the scabbard. After he killed him, he cut off his head with the sword.

1 Samuel 17:4,8,16,26,40,45,48-51 (NIV)

David was a brave young man. He knew that his God was greater than anything he faced. Although David was an anointed king — and had certainly found favor in God's eye — he faced numerous obstacles throughout his lifetime, one of which was Saul's opposition toward him. Suddenly the one who called for David to play his harp to bring peace and rest to his troubled soul was now after him to take his life. Why? Because Saul became jealous of David.

The Bible says that jealousy is as cruel as the grave, and it certainly is (Song of Solomon 8:6). Jealousy, in its extreme state, will cause a person to take (or attempt to take) another's life. Jealousy can also destroy one mentally, emotionally, and even spiritually. Saul's jealousy developed as a result of David being attributed greater worth than himself. A song was written by the Israelite women in praise of David and his accomplishments.

As they danced, they sang: "Saul has slain his thousands, and David his tens of thousands."

Saul was very angry; this refrain galled him. "They have credited David with tens of thousands," he thought,

"but me with only thousands. What more can he get but the kingdom?"

And from that time on Saul kept a jealous eye on David.

1 Samuel 18:7-9 (NIV)

You see, Saul was really afraid that David would rise above him in power and in favor with the people. Saul's jealousy really stemmed from the fact that the Lord was with David but had left him. Not only was he jealous of David, but he was fearful of him. Saul witnessed David's *great success* in everything he did. This was because the anointing of God was upon David. What does that say to us? If we stay within the parameters God has outlined for our lives and "walk in the Spirit," we too will experience great success.

All too often people become jealous because they feel threatened by another's success and abilities. This should not be an acceptable practice in the body of Christ. Every believer should strive to *please God* to the best of his or her ability but not as though competing with another. This leads us to another obstacle in the body, the "spirit of competition."

The "Spirit of Competition" — Competition is "The act of competing: rivalry, contest, match."[11]

The "spirit of competition" causes one to feel that he or she is better than the other person or can do a particular thing better than the other person and, therefore, seeks to prove *that*. I am not referring to the harmless type of competition that we sometimes see as part of our church events, the kind that takes place for fun and entertainment, and to promote achievement and growth. I am referring to the kind of competition that is induced by "self" or worse yet, influenced by carnal, selfish, and ungodly motives. I believe that those who feel the need to compete within the body of Christ are actually insecure within themselves and lack confidence in God. Competition also takes place among those who are "greedy" of position, some sort of gain, or favor.

One who operates under the umbrella of competing, operates out of his or her own self. In the kingdom of God, there is no room for this kind of competing. One who competes does so to prove and promote himself or herself. But we know that promotion comes from God (Psalm 75:6,7).

The "spirit of competition" has carnal roots. The Word of God lets us know that anyone who professes to be a Christian but operates with a carnal mind, is an enemy of God.

For to be carnally minded is death; but to be spiritually minded is life and peace.

Because the carnal mind is enmity against God: for it is not subject to the law of God, neither indeed can be.

So then they that are in the flesh cannot please God.

But ye are not in the flesh, but in the Spirit, if so be that the Spirit of God dwell in you. Now if any man have not the Spirit of Christ, he is none of his.

And if Christ be in you, the body is dead because of sin; but the Spirit is life because of righteousness.

Romans 8:6-10

Competition that is driven by envy and jealousy in the body of Christ is carnal. It is of the flesh! The works of the flesh will kill us — cause spiritual death — if we let it rule us. As women of God, we must walk in the Spirit *and be led by the Spirit* in order to come out of self. The "spirit of competition" also has satanic roots. Satan loves to see those in the body of Christ competing *against* one another for status, position, and reputation. This kind of competition is destructive not only to the one operating under that "spirit," but also to others. Let's be sure that our motives are right no matter what we do.

Painful Emotions — Painful emotions are those things in one's life that cannot be shared with anyone. They are feelings that develop as a result of negative, even traumatic experiences. Those feelings lodge deep in the spirit of the individual as a constant reminder of that incident or experience and set themselves up as a hindrance and barrier to the emotional, spiritual, and mental growth of an individual.

Such events/traumas as rape and abuse (verbal and physical) have painful emotional consequences on women in general, and many women in the body of Christ have experienced rape and abuse. Many Christian women experienced these things before becoming a Christian, but sadly, it also happens to Christian women as well. Becoming a Christian alone doesn't remove the painful reality of those experiences. One must allow God to heal those emotions and this — my sister — is not easy, and it takes time.

Since rape and abuse are highlights of this section, I would like to look more closely at them beginning with their definitions.

Rape — "The crime of forcing a person to submit to sexual intercourse. The act of seizing and carrying off by force."[12]

Abuse — "To use wrongfully or improperly. To maltreat. To attack with insults."[13]

I can't imagine anything more painful than rape. The fact that one violates someone else's body by *forcing* that person to engage in sexual intercourse against her (even his) will or desire is inhuman. Rape is a brutal, selfish act against another's will.

Not only is rape a violation of one's rights but now the person who has been raped becomes tied to the rapist just by the mere fact that intercourse has taken place. What do I mean? Sexual intercourse is the ultimate giving of oneself. Somehow, it emotionally links the two people together. Even in relationships that end in separation of the two people, and where rape is not a factor — it is often difficult for one to discontinue his or her affair with the other person because they have become emotionally tied together. Even when the relationship ends, thoughts and desires continue to linger for each other.

When a woman's sexual rights are violated she receives a transfer of spirits from the violator whether she wants to or not. The one being violated becomes "uncovered." This is why God forbids His people time and time again to intermarry or intermingle (have sexual relationships) with those from other nations or those serving "other gods."

When two people become sexually intimate they become one body. "What? Know ye not that he which is joined to an harlot is one body? For two, saith he, shall be one flesh" (1 Corinthians 6:16). The word "joined" in this regard means, "to keep company with." The one who keeps company with a harlot becomes one with her, that is, one in spirit. They become alike. The spirit of an individual enters from one person to another through the act of intercourse. This is why God ordained marriage. Sexual activity should only be shared between husband and wife because more takes place during intercourse than just the physical aspect of it. Thus, it is important that one allows God to choose his or her mate.

In my own words, rape simply means to take by force — uncovering one's sexuality — without consent! For example, Tamar was raped by her brother Amnon. Let's look at the account.

> And Amnon was so vexed, that he fell sick for his sister Tamar; for she was a virgin; and Amnon thought it hard for him to do anything to her.
>
> So Amnon lay down, and made himself sick: and when the king was come to see him, Amnon said unto the king, I pray thee, let Tamar my sister come, and make me a couple of cakes in my sight, that I may eat at her hand.
>
> Then David sent home to Tamar, saying, Go now to thy brother Amnon's house, and dress him meat.
>
> So Tamar went to her brother Amnon's house; and he was laid down. And she took flour, and kneaded it, and made cakes in his sight, and did bake the cakes.
>
> And Amnon said unto Tamar, Bring the meat into the chamber, that I may eat of thine hand. And Tamar took the cakes which she had made, and brought them into the chamber to Amnon her brother.

And when she had brought them unto him to eat, he took hold of her [grabbed her], and said unto her, Come lie with me, my sister.

And she answered him, Nay, my brother, *do not force me*....

Howbeit he would not hearken unto her voice: but, being stronger than she, forced her, and lay with her. [The NIV says, But he refused to listen to her, and since he was stronger than she, he raped her.]

Then Amnon hated her exceedingly; so that the hatred wherewith he hated her was greater than the love wherewith he had loved her. And Amnon said unto her, Arise, be gone.
                                    2 Samuel 13:2,6-8,10-12,14,15

In these verses, rapists are referred to as "wicked fools." In spiritual rape, Satan does everything possible to take by force those things that God has given you and placed in your care as sacred. He wants to strip you and "uncover" you. You, however, must take those things back by force! How can this be done? Through spiritual warfare such as was discussed in chapter one. Don't let Satan violate your rights as a woman of God. Don't let him intrude on your property!

Abuse is another brutal, uncompassionate act from one person toward another. Physical abuse is rampant in our society even within the bonds of marriage. Yes, even in Christian homes! If not physical abuse, then verbal abuse is often present. Physical and verbal abuse scar an individual. It leaves a mark, a lingering sign of damage that is sometimes irreparable. It breaks the very spirit and emotions of an individual. We see all kinds of abuse — among all kinds of people — in this sin-infested world that we live in. God is not pleased!!

In my opinion, abuse is a blatant, merciless, and uncompassionate disrespect of one's feelings, efforts, and expressed thoughts. The abuser has no genuine feelings for or respect of the individual he or she is abusing, his or her needs are most important. I believe abuse is an expression of anger.

81

Abuse, like rape, is an act inspired by Satan himself. If you are being intolerably abused emotionally — or abused physically in any way — get help!

I feel the need to mention that *some* abusers have more than likely been abused — in some way — themselves and they too need help. The fact that they have been abused, however, does not, at all, justify their abusive tendencies.

I have learned by studying/researching, observing, and listening to those who have experienced rape and abuse, that women who have endured such pain tend to store those experiences in their emotions. By doing this, they can hide them from others, but at the same time, hold on to them and nurture them for times when they feel worthless and perhaps fall into situations that resemble these past experiences, for times when they feel most vulnerable. Sometimes the "worthless" feeling serves as a validation to these women that they can feed on their past experiences even if they are negative. These women then develop "hiding places" to cover their pain. These "hiding places," however, are only temporary distractions to the pain; they don't actually remove the pain or erase the experience. Such "hiding places" could be *excessive* shopping, eating, watching television, working, or such the like. In other words, "hiding places" are those areas that bring temporary enjoyment to an individual, those areas which help one to seemingly escape the pain and memory of his or her experiences. The notion is that if one can fill his or her life with everything else, there won't be time to think about these painful areas.

However, the way to overcome these painful emotions is to confront them. One must be willing to acknowledge his or her pain and fears before the healing can begin. Healing can take place through many avenues such as counseling, confrontation, and prayer. If one seeks help outside of the church, he or she should make sure that it is with someone (or an organization) that is credible, reputable, reliable, trustworthy, and has been established for a while. If counseling is sought within the church — which is preferable for

Christians because one needs to connect with those who are like-minded, and believes that the Bible has a remedy for all of life's circumstances through the power of God — be sure it is with a Bible-believing, Spirit-filled, trustworthy man or woman of God, whether it's your pastor or some other notable person within the body of Christ. Most of all, search the Word of God concerning your situation, and pray for God's direction.

Your problem is not too hard or big for God. He is the master physician specializing in healing bruised emotions and broken hearts or spirits. As a matter of fact, the Word of God tells us that a broken and contrite heart He will not despise (Psalm 51:17). Whether you are broken because of sin or through relationships with others, God will not despise you. Yield yourself to God, tell *all* to Him and let the healing begin.

The Spirit of Fear — Fear is, "A feeling of alarm or disquiet caused by awareness of or expectation of danger. To be apprehensive (fearful, uneasy)."[14]

According to *Vine's Complete Expository Dictionary of Old and New Testament Words*, fear is terror. "It seems best to understand it as that which is caused by the intimidation of adversaries."[15]

First of all, it is important that you understand that fear does not come from God. It comes from the adversary of your soul, Satan. Fear can also come from lack of confidence in God and in oneself. I use the term "spirit of fear" to identify that negative type of fear that comes from the devil. But I am not talking about the kind of fear that one experiences occasionally when venturing into something new. We know that God has not given us the spirit of fear, but of love, power, and a sound mind (2 Timothy 1:7). Yet, we allow the enemy to enclose us in fear. Satan is constantly trying to captivate us in areas that God has already delivered us from or areas in which God will greatly use us. These are not necessarily areas of sin but rather areas of insecurity, immaturity, and areas in which we lack understanding. Satan uses fear as a "stronghold" against God's people.

Fear often enters our lives because we are not as strong and confident in God as we should be. It is, therefore, important that we develop a strong relationship with God, making Him a part of everything we do. We need to understand that Jesus Christ died not only for our sins but also for our mental and emotional liberation. Fear binds, not frees! In other words, fear limits or hinders an individual. Fear works on the mind! But we are encouraged in God's Word that we:

> **...have not received the spirit of bondage again to fear; but ye have received the Spirit of adoption, whereby we cry, Abba, Father.**
>
> **Romans 8:15**

In the spirit realm, a person who is bound by fear can only see their weaknesses, frailties, inabilities, and insecurities. He or she feels as though there is no defense against whatever attacks the enemy has launched. This person often feels trapped, as if there is no way out. Fear is controlling; it drives a person, clouds normal thought patterns, and begins to cause some of the following:

- Anxiety
- Panic
- Nervousness
- Paranoia (or delusions)
- Torment ("a source of harassment or pain"[16])
- Uneasiness (inability to relax)
- Sleeplessness
- Incapacitates ("to deprive of strength or ability; disable"[17])
- Worry ("to feel or cause to feel uneasy or troubled"[18])
- Defeat
- Mental and emotional instability

Fear manifests itself into various phobias. Such as:

- Heights (Acrophobia)

- Open spaces (Agoraphobia)
- Enclosed spaces (Claustrophobia)
- Death (Necrophobia)
- Night or darkness (Nyctophobia)
- Crowds (Ochlophobia)
- Noise (Phonophobia)
- Love (Erotophobia)

Fear can make one feel as if he or she is going crazy. Fear can drive one to react "out of control." The "spirit of fear" debilitates and incapacitates to the degree that one begins to see, hear, feel, and believe the existence of a mere shadow, an illusion. Circumstances are blown out of proportion in the mind of the individual who is captivated by fear. If we look at the word "illusion," we see that it is "an erroneous perception of reality. An erroneous concept or belief, a misleading visual image."[19] For the believer, such an image is seen in the "spirit world" and is that which others cannot see in the natural realm. In other words, Satan will even use fear to play tricks on one's mind.

You may ask, "How can fear cause one to visualize that which isn't true or real?" Remember, as Christians our fight is spiritual. We are not wrestling against flesh and blood, but instead we are battling principalities, powers, and demonic spirits (Ephesians 6:12). Therefore, Satan can play on one's mind causing him or her to have illusions or visualize those things that tangibly don't exist in the natural realm but exist in the spirit realm. That's why it's important for us to be able to make a distinction between what is real and what is not real, what is of God and what is of the devil, and what is demonic activity.

My sister, Satan wants you to believe a lie! He wants you to see what's not really there. He wants to put fear in your life to put you on the run even when there's nothing or no one to run from. Understand that fear is very real and has gripping powers that can destroy an individual, powers that can only be broken by the Word of God. The "spirit of fear" is very real but it can be broken by the very real power of God!

Fear will paralyze you spiritually, if you let it overtake you. Satan comes in so many different ways to kill, steal, and destroy (John 10:10). He often plots against God's people in ways that he knows will cause devastation and public humiliation. In other words, he tries to discredit God through his attacks against His people. First John 4:18 tells us that perfect love casts out fear. We know that God is love and that once we have Him *in* our lives, there should be no room for this kind of fear. Yes, we may become anxious at times when we are faced with challenges (good or bad), but we should never be captivated and controlled by fear.

I believe that the only way to get rid of fear is with the Word of God. A constant recitation and confession of God's Word as it relates to fear will drive fear out. Once you fill your life with the Word of God, your confidence in God will be strengthened, and the Word in you will show up the devil for who he really is — a defeated foe. Satan goes about *as* a roaring lion (1 Peter 5:8). What you need to understand is that he is only functioning in his role as "the great pretender." He isn't actually a lion; he just pretends to be one. The key is for you to stay in God's protection. God has fully-equipped you to defeat Satan's schemes.

> **...the one who is in you is greater than the one who is in the world.**
>
> **1 John 4:4 (NIV)**

The "spirit of fear" is a strategic attack from the enemy to literally kill you. If Satan can get you to think you're a nobody, you will never rise up to be what God wants you to be. Not only will he entice you to believe a lie, but he'll get you to confess it until you receive it in your spirit, and then he'll get you to act on it.

My Personal Battle With Fear

In the summer of 1980, I began attending Bethel Tabernacle Pentecostal Church in the South End of Boston, Massachusetts. During that year I was baptized in the "saving name" of Jesus (Acts 4:12) and was filled with the Holy Spirit. Prior to this I did not have a personal relationship with God, although I believed in God. I was a much younger woman at the time I received Christ but was (and still am) very serious about serving God. I certainly didn't know what God had in store for me down through the years, but I believe that Satan knew, so he launched an attack of fear against me.

Almost immediately after I was saved, the enemy cast a "spirit of fear" over my life. At the time, I did not know what was happening to me, but as I matured in God, I soon realized that it was one of Satan's devices against me to kill me. I don't use the word "kill" lightly either. Satan is out to kill, steal, and destroy the people of God, especially if he sees potential in them (John 10:10). Satan does not target anyone who does not pose a threat against his kingdom.

I began to experience tremendous anxiety and apprehension in my life. I was uneasy and on edge all the time. It was a terrible feeling and I knew it wasn't from God. I experienced an anxious-type of care about everything, no matter how small or great. My life suddenly was filled with fear for no apparent reason. Fear began to affect me spiritually, emotionally, academically, and even physically. After God delivered me, I realized the "spirit of fear" was one of Satan's attack against me because I had given my life to Christ — no longer to serve sin.

Fear literally "gripped" me. It had a "stronghold" on my life. My sister, this was the worst experience I had ever gone through! I would not wish it on my worst enemy. But thanks be to God who gave me the victory! The "spirit of fear" even interfered with my sleep patterns. Many nights I would lay awake unable to sleep. My heart was filled with fear! Yes, I even experienced heart palpitations, something I had never experienced before. Some may call this anxiety attacks, but I know it was the devil.

My weight began to drop rapidly. I was already thin. At one point, my doctor had to place me on a special milkshake diet so that I could regain my weight. Although others (including my doctor) speculated about what was happening to me, no one knew what I was feeling, or what I was going through on the inside, no one but God. God is always there no matter what! I know for sure that God will be with His people during their worst tests.

My mom — who at the time wasn't saved — thought I was going to die. I cried constantly, mostly, from being "afraid," not knowing what was happening to me. During this time, I did not know what the criteria was for one having a nervous breakdown, but, looking back, I believe that's exactly where I was headed (or at least where Satan wished I was headed). Do you see how Satan works? His ultimate purpose was not just to paralyze me with fear, his purpose was to bring on all types of conditions and symptoms as a result of fear. He planted the seed of fear; and as that seed grew, its roots spread into other areas of my life. I began to experience things that I never even imagined I ever would. Nonetheless, God was my fortress and strong tower. I found safety and refuge in Him alone.

Satan was limited because God only allowed him to do so much to me. I believe that God said the same thing to Satan about me as He did concerning Job. You see, I loved God with all my heart, soul, and might. I wanted to be saved and stay saved no matter what the cost and I believe this was my test. I could hear God saying to Satan, "Touch all that she has and even touch her body but don't touch her life." God had not given Satan permission to take my life.

During this time I felt that I had no power whatsoever, even though the Spirit of God lived on the inside. I felt hopeless and helpless. But in fact, in my weakness, God showed His strength. Satan didn't wait until I became a mature Christian to attack me. He attacked me in my infancy. Nevertheless, God brought me out. This experience forced me to dive into God's Word for myself. It was through this experience and my desire to serve God that I learned the power of the Word of God!

God's Word is what finally delivered me from the "spirit of fear." When I couldn't sleep at nights, I read the Word of God. I filled my spirit so much with the Word that I could quote Scripture after Scripture by verbatim, but it was more than just quoting Scripture. I developed a dependence on God's Word. I ate it for breakfast, lunch, dinner, and a mid-night snack. I took Psalm 1:2 literally. I meditated on God's Word day and night, night and day. No matter where I went or what I was doing, God's Word was in my heart and thoughts. My fight against the "spirit of fear" seemed like it went on forever and ever (probably about 6 to 8 months in reality). As a babe in Christ, this was a tremendous obstacle for me to overcome. Many times I wondered if I would overcome it, or it would overcome me.

Some of my favorite Scriptures at that time were: Psalm 1, Isaiah 26:3, Isaiah 41:10,13,14, Isaiah 42:6, Isaiah 43:1,2,4,5, 2 Timothy 1:7, and Psalm 118:6.

John declared that once a person knows the "truth," that truth would set him or her free (John 8:32). I have proved this to be true. God's Word is truth, and if you fill your life with this truth it will deliver you — no matter what the circumstance! In John 14:6 Jesus declared, "I am the way, the truth, and the life...." Before I knew it, I was delivered. All the symptoms associated with fear had left me. My life started coming back together again. I was truly free indeed!

You may feel bound by the "spirit of fear," but don't give up. God can and will deliver you. Remember, the only way to be delivered from fear is through the Word of God. Fill your life with the Word. Confess it and believe it every opportunity you get. Heaven and earth will pass away, but the Word of God is sure (Matthew 24:35). It will stand under the most intense pressures in your life.

As women of God our individual prayer should be, "Lord, help me to be a woman of character, integrity, and self-worth — no matter what my struggles are. I know that as long as I have you in my life, I will experience deliverance, victory, and success."

[1] *The Merriam Webster Dictionary*, p. 106.

[2] *The Merriam Webster Dictionary*, p. 106.

[3] *The Merriam Webster Dictionary*, p. 362.

[4] *The Merriam Webster Dictionary*, p. 90.

[5] *The Merriam Webster Dictionary*, p. 624.

[6] *The Merriam Webster Dictionary*, p. 255.

[7] *The Merriam Webster Dictionary*, p. 402.

[8] *The Full Life Study Bible New International Version* (Life Publishers International, 1992), p. 1944.

[9] *The American Heritage Dictionary*, pp. 629,630.

[10] W.E. Vine, Merrill F. Unger, and William White, Jr., *Vine's Complete Expository Dictionary of Old and New Testament Words* (Nashville: Thomas Nelson, Inc., Publishers, 1996), p. 5.

[11] *The Merriam Webster Dictionary*, p. 164.

[12] *The American Heritage Dictionary*, p. 569.

[13] *The American Heritage Dictionary*, p. 3.

[14] *The American Heritage Dictionary*, p. 257.

[15] Vine, Unger, and White, p. 230.

[16] *The American Heritage Dictionary*, p. 714.

[17] *The American Heritage Dictionary*, p. 350.

[18] *The American Heritage Dictionary*, p. 786.

[19] *The American Heritage Dictionary*, pp. 344,345.

Chapter 5
Women of the Word

The Bible tells us that heaven and earth will pass away but God's Word will never pass away (Matthew 24:35). The phrase "heaven and earth will pass away" simply means that there is nothing lasting or of permanent value on this earth. Everything we see with our natural eyes will one day pass away. Everything we know in relation to this earthly realm will pass away. All of our possessions will pass away. The only thing that will last is the Word of God. Jesus' response to Satan when he tempted Him in the wilderness to command that the stones be turned to bread was, "It is written, Man shall not live by bread alone, but by every word that proceedeth out of the mouth of God" (Matthew 4:4).

As Christians, God's Word is a vital source of our existence. It is the Word of God that defines who we are. Therefore, it behooves us to study God's Word, believe in it, and be doers of it, not just hearers (James 1:22-25).

One might ask, "What is it about God's Word that makes it sure?" The Word is the essence of God and His character. His Word describes His nature and His desires. The Word of God is forever settled in heaven (Psalm 119:89).

The Word of God is:

- God Himself (John 1:1).
- Inclusive of His nature.
- Inclusive of His existence; His being.
- Inclusive of His awesome power.

- Inclusive of His love for humankind (John 3:16).
- Inclusive of His creative ability (Genesis 1).
- Inclusive of His mercy (Exodus 34:6-7).
- Inclusive of His grace (John 1:17, Galatians 1:15,16).
- Inclusive of His divinity.
- Inclusive of His forgiveness (Ephesians 1:7, Colossians 1:14).
- Inclusive of His Lordship.
- Inclusive of His preeminence (Colossians 1:16-23).
- Inclusive of His will and desire for humankind.
- Inclusive of His salvation (Ephesians 2:8,9).

God's Word is our primary source. It is our lifeline. We cannot live spiritually without God or His Word just as we cannot live without food and water. One can only live for so long without food and water. Without food and water for a certain length of time one would become physically weak and vulnerable to all kinds of sickness and disease.

If the body isn't replenished with food and water, it will eventually die. The same principle applies spiritually. If we don't feed on the Word of God, we will become weak and susceptible to all manner of spiritual attacks sent by the devil. The only way to combat these attacks is to fill ourselves with the Word of God, pray and do those things that contribute to a healthy Christian life on a daily basis.

Through reading God's Word one can increase his or her faith in God and His promises, thereby rejecting and resisting the attacks of the enemy. In fact, the only way to activate and increase our faith is by receiving the Word of God. Romans 10:17 (NIV) declares that "…faith comes from hearing the message, and the message is heard through the word of Christ."

We must desire to know God's thoughts and expression. There are two ways in which we can know God and His Word, (1) *Logos* and (2) *Rhema*. I believe we must seek to understand and know God in both aspects. Can one truly know the mind of God? I believe that we all can reach a place in God where we know and understand His will for our lives, and thus know the mind of God.

Vine's Complete Expository Dictionary of Old and New Testament Words shares the following about logos and rhema:

> **Logos** — "The Word. 'The Personal Word,' a title of the Son of God."[1] See John 1:1-18.

> **The Word** [God] **became flesh** [Jesus] **and made his dwelling among us....**
> **John 1:14 (NIV)**

> **Rhema** — "Denotes that which is spoken, what is uttered in speech or writing. Rhema, an utterance, the articulated expression of a thought."[2] The words that proceed out of the mouth of God.

"The logos is the distinct and superinfinite personality of God; His deity; His creative power; His incarnation ("became flesh"); and His glory."[3] Creation was made by the rhema ("utterance") of God. "Logos is reasoned speech, rhema an utterance; the articulated expression of thought."[4]

What does this all mean? It means that women of the Word will not only invest time in the written Word (Bible), but will also seek and listen for a divine utterance or expression of thought from God, in other words, the revealed Word of God in one's heart or spirit. I call it the "quickened" word in one's spirit.

As women of God, we don't want to be weak and feeble-minded Christians. We don't want to become spiritually dehydrated from lack of the Word. Therefore, it is imperative that we become "women of the Word." In other words, we need a divine impartation from God out of the abundance of His storehouse, such as Moses received many times concerning his position and authority to lead God's people. We need to be replenished and revived by the Word of God.

Let me interject here that it is not enough just to know the Bible (by memory). One must also put into practice the teachings of the Bible. I believe this can only be done through the aid or assistance of the Holy Spirit. There are too many people (including non-Christians) who know the Bible inside out, yet have not committed to a life lived in obedience to its teachings. Head knowledge is not enough! Your heart must be knitted to God's Word.

The Word of God gives us insight into life's circumstances and situations. It gives us a "heads up" to what's coming. It prepares us for life's challenges and gives solutions and advice that will work! I believe that once a Christian reaches and maintains a certain level of maturity and quality of relationship with God, God will begin to share and reveal more of Himself to that individual. God — the Holy Spirit — will become an aid to that person. Far too long have we gone to others seeking advice and counsel only to find that others are struggling with the same problems that we struggle with. I am not implying that people can't give counsel while going through their own problems. I am simply saying that it would be better for us to go to God in prayer first. If we need advice from others, let God direct us to a strong, Spirit-filled counselor.

God wants you to cast your cares on Him because He cares for you (1 Peter 5:7). Such care is known as God's providence. God wants continual involvement in your life. God's providence over you includes preservation through His Word and provision — both physically and naturally — by His Word (Philippians 4:19).

How can we ensure God's providence over our lives? We can do so by obeying His *revealed will* for our lives. How will we know His revealed will? By reading, studying, and obeying His Word which contains His will for us. It is especially true in the times that we are living in that we must constantly be in tune with God's will for our lives as we serve Him and minister to others in His name.

What Does it Mean To Be Women of the Word?

It means to be women who love to read, study, and live according to the Word of God. Women of the Word are those who put aside their own ways, intellect, and desires in order that they may be governed by the Word of God. They are women who hunger and thirst after righteousness, that is, the righteousness of God, not self-righteousness. For we know that our own righteousness is as filthy rags.

Do your best to present yourself to God as one approved, a workman who does not need to be ashamed and who correctly handles the word of truth.
2 Timothy 2:15 (NIV)

In order to be women of the Word, we must become familiar with God's Word. We must read it, embrace it, believe it, confess it, share it, trust it, live it, and love it. When one loves something, he or she spends a lot of time with that particular thing or person. There is a constant desire to be around that thing or person. There is an attraction to that thing that causes the individual to spend hours upon hours with it.

Some spend hours and hours before the television, on the internet, in the shopping malls, and so on. We must be the same way with God's Word. We must become dependent on the Word to the degree that we can't live from day to day without it. We must grow to love God's Word and develop an appreciation for it. After all, we learn the character and mind of God through His Word. This only comes through an intimate relationship and constant fellowship with God.

Those who desire to be led by God must desire His Word. God is the Word (John 1:1). There is only one way to know what God's will is for your life and that's through His Word. A life that's filled with the Word of God is filled with power, assurance, confidence, victory, joy, peace, love, forgiveness, and the saving grace of God.

Women of the Word are fruitful and productive in the service of the Lord. They are the ones God can entrust and bestow blessings upon. They are the ones who will take the one talent that God has given them and use it faithfully to serve others and God until He multiplies it.

Let us strive to be women of the Word. It is equally important that we are teachable and that we take advantage of every opportunity to learn more about God's Word through others who have invested time and prayer in God's Word so we can continue to grow and help others.

The Word of God must become a need, not just a mere want. Our need should be based on the following facts about God's Word.

- It stands firm in the heavens (Psalm 119:89-91, Isaiah 40:8, 1 Peter 1:24,25).
- It is powerful (Hebrews 4:12).
- It has power to create (Psalm 33:6-9, Hebrews 11:3,Genesis 1:1,3,6,11).
- It sustains creation (Psalm 147:15-18).
- It makes us holy (John 17:17).
- It is our weapon against the enemy (Ephesians 6:10-17).

As I close out this chapter, I offer the following ways in which Christian women can begin to position themselves in regards to the Word of God. Position yourself to receive from God. If you desire to operate in the divine will of God as a mature Christian woman you must:

- Seek to understand the Word of God (Matthew 13:23).
- Totally trust in the Word (Psalm 119:42).
- Obey its instructions (Psalm 119:17,67, James 1:22-24).
- Live by it (Psalm 119:9).
- Hope in its promises (Psalm 119:74,81,114; 130:5).
- Love it (Psalm 119:47,113).
- Offer praise to God for His Word (Psalm 56:4,10).

Placing focus on these and other areas, with a sincere desire to please God, will definitely bring about positive results in one's life. Finally, I would like to leave with you this simple, yet effective, formula that God placed in my spirit one day as I was preparing a Bible lesson.

Faith + The Word of God = Explosive Power!

Your faith mixed with the Word of God will bring not only victory and deliverance in your life, but also in the lives of those you touch. When you combine your faith with God's Word you make a no-risk investment that is guaranteed to give you a 100 percent return. In the natural realm, God's Word even demonstrates how the rain and the snow come down from heaven to water the earth and to make it bud and flourish. In the spiritual realm,

> **So is my word that goes out from my mouth: It will not return to me empty, but will accomplish what I desire and achieve the purpose for which I sent it.**

> **Isaiah 55:11 (NIV)**

[1, 2, 3, 4] W.E. Vine, Merrill F. Unger, and William White, Jr., *Vine's Complete Expository Dictionary of Old and New Testament Words* (Nashville: Thomas Nelson, Inc., Publishers, 1996), p. 683.

Chapter 6
God, Are You Calling Me?

Knowing the Voice of God

In order for us to answer the call of God in our lives, we must know, be able to detect, and distinguish His voice. Let's look at the Gospel of John and his account of the good shepherd and the sheep.

> Verily, verily I say unto you, He that entereth not by the door into the sheepfold, but climbeth up some other way, the same is a thief and a robber.
>
> But he that entereth in by the door is the shepherd of the sheep.
>
> To him the porter openeth; and the sheep hear his voice: and he calleth his own sheep by name, and leadeth them out.
>
> And when he putteth forth his own sheep, he goeth before them, and the sheep follow him: for they know his voice.
>
> And a stranger will they not follow, but will flee from him: for they know not the voice of strangers.
>
> I am the good shepherd, and know my sheep, and am known of mine.
>
> John 10:1-5,14

We too must be confident and secure in our relationship with God and desire to know Him just as He knows us.

How can this be done? Through communication, which is a vital part of our relationship with God. Communication not only affects us in earthly matters, but in matters of the spirit as well. There are two main avenues by which one can communicate. First, communication involves speaking, and second, it involves listening. Speaking has two mediums: (1) verbal articulation and (2) the written word. One's written word is just as binding a representation as a verbal expression.

As believers, we should exercise our ability to listen and strive to understand the language of the Spirit which I believe can only be done through prayer or can be understood through prayer. I learned in a course I took called Communicating Across Cultures that there are different distances by which we communicate. The instructor shared that in the western culture, for example, there are four zones that define/describe the physical distance by which people communicate with each other.

1. **Intimate Zone** — A distance of zero to eighteen inches (0"-18") between two people. This space is usually reserved for family and/or spouse.

2. **Personal Zone** — A distance of one and one half to four feet ($1\frac{1}{2}$'-4') between two people. This space is reserved for general conversations between two people.

3. **Social Zone** — A distance of four to ten feet (4'-10'). This space is reserved for social gatherings.

4. **Public Zone** — A distance of ten to twelve feet (10'-12') between people. This space is reserved for lectures, performances, Sunday morning sermons, and so on.

I used the above illustration only to provide a more vivid picture — perhaps of something we can relate to better — and contrast how communication happens between people as opposed to how it happens between God and humankind. I am by no means suggesting or implying that God is confined or limited to our boundaries.

In matters of the Spirit, God desires to communicate with His people by entering their "intimate zone." This, of course, can only happen as we develop and build a relationship of intimacy with God. One must welcome, allow, and even entice the Spirit of God to come into that "intimate zone" before He actually will.

There are some Christians who are comfortable relating to God in their "personal zone." Anything closer than this becomes uncomfortable for them because their relationship with God has not fully developed or matured. In order to relate to God on an "intimate" level, we must yield to His will for our lives. Because some find it difficult to completely yield to God, they relate to God at a distance. Yet, God tugs at our heart through the Holy Spirit. When we ignore or reject that tug, we are saying to God — in essence — "I don't want to let you in my life," or "I don't want you to govern my life." We draw close to God only when we need Him to act on our behalf — because we feel secure having control over our own lives as opposed to submitting to God and allowing Him to control our lives.

No Spirit-filled, Bible-believing Christian who recognizes God's call on his or her life should communicate with God in the parameters of a "public," "social," or even "personal" zone. God wants intimacy with His people! It is only then that He can share more of Himself, and we can receive more of Him.

When the angel Gabriel appeared to Mary to tell her that she would give birth to the Savior of the world, she found it hard to believe because of the way in which she would conceive. (This conception would not be by natural means, but by the Holy Spirit). (See Luke 1:28-32).

When God speaks, He gets to the heart of the matter! What an honor this was for Mary. God came into Mary's life in a very intimate, powerful way, and that's the way He wants to come into your life. Let Him in.

God speaks in many ways. He speaks directly through His Word. He speaks to the inner person (spirit or heart) of an individual. He speaks through others (prophets, preachers, teachers). He speaks through natural causes. Through whatever medium God chooses to speak, we need to get to the place where we "know (recognize) His voice" undoubtedly and without hesitation.

Believers often reject or delay to respond to the voice of God because they don't recognize His voice. In other words, they aren't sure it's Him. Or, they are not confident enough in their relationship with God to know His voice. Be honest; a lot of times when you hear God speak within, you begin to rationalize with yourself because you think that it is you speaking and not God. In other words, you think that whatever is said, comes from what you are feeling, thinking, or what you know. Things only appear to be unclear when we try to use our own understanding or intellect to deal with matters of the Spirit.

We tend to look at our frailties, failures, inadequacies, and inabilities. God, on the other hand, sees the finished product. He doesn't look at what we are (present tense); He looks at what we can become (future tense).

Some reject God's call or run away from it because they feel unqualified and undeserving. Questions begin to surface such as, "Why would you want to use me in this area?" or "I'm not equipped for this task" or "But Lord, you don't understand that my life is not where it should be — you can't use me." We make excuses just as Moses did when God called him to deliver the children of Israel out of Egypt. Here is the account.

"So now, go. I [God] am sending you [Moses] to Pharaoh to bring my people the Israelites out of Egypt."

But Moses said to God, "Who am I, that I should go to Pharaoh and bring the Israelites out of Egypt?"

And God said, "I will be with you. And this will be the sign to you that it is I who have sent you: When you have brought the people out of Egypt, you will worship God on this mountain."

Moses said to God, "Suppose I go to the Israelites and say to them, 'The God of your fathers has sent me to you,' and they ask me, 'What is his name?' Then what shall I tell them?"

God said to Moses, "I AM WHO I AM. This is what you are to say to the Israelites: 'I AM has sent me to you.'"

Moses answered, "What if they do not believe me or listen to me and say, 'The Lord did not appear to you'?"

Moses said to the Lord, "O Lord, I have never been eloquent, neither in the past nor since you have spoken to your servant. I am slow of speech and tongue."

"Now go; I [God] will help you speak and will teach you what to say."

But Moses said, "O Lord, please send someone else to do it."

Exodus 3:10-14; 4:1,10,12,13 (NIV)

Doesn't this sound like us? For every excuse that Moses made, God gave a solution. Although we might feel unequipped for what God has called us to do, we can be assured that God will help us when it's time to speak, and He'll teach us what to say. In addition, God often calls us to specific tasks that coincide with the spiritual gifts and abilities He has already given us. This should make our task a little easier because we have the assistance of God, through the gifts that He has placed in us.

Think about it. When God extended His saving grace to you, He immediately began working on you to shape you and prepare you for what He would require of you as a "mature" Christian. Many of us don't realize that God has been allowing us to go through processes since the day we decided to serve Him. Whatever process you are going through or have been through, begin to thank God for it. You can't see it now, but it's working out for your good (Romans 8:28). It will shape you, give you stamina, define you, and give you character. It is important for you to understand that God never requires of you anything you are unable to produce or deliver.

God — the Holy Spirit — comes alongside you as your helper (John 14:16-18,26). Yes, it's often difficult to see where you will end up and how you will get there, but rest assured, God knows, and He is with you every step of the way to see you through.

If you are in constant fellowship with God, nothing should really take you by surprise. God always gives hints and inclinations about what He is about to do in one's life. I'm sure you can look back over your life at areas in which God has already used you. At the time, these areas probably seemed to you to be insignificant, general, basic, and without future implications. In other words, usually people start out in a different area of ministry from what God will ultimately call them to do, but I believe that these areas are links to help prepare them for that particular task. If you really examine God's work in your life, you'll notice that these areas link together to form something greater, more specific, and focused (task-oriented) in you. For many, God uses the seemingly smaller arenas to elevate them to a greater purpose and call. Working for God is an honor. Nothing is insignificant in the kingdom of God!

This is probably the best place for me to pause and define the word "call."

Call — "To cry or utter loudly or clearly. To **summon**. To name; **designate**. To **consider**."[1]

It is very clear, based on the definition above, that one who is "called" has been given a charge, a summons (Isaiah 43:1). When God calls you, that call is clear because the Spirit speaks expressly (clearly). He speaks a specific, distinct, and precise word that is focused or concentrated on a particular area or task. Remember, God is the one that does the calling. It is a divine call. Let's look, for example, at how God placed certain ministries (offices) in the church. Remember, the ministries belong to God not to man. This means that one cannot ultimately prevent another from functioning in a particular office that God has placed him or her in, merely because that individual may not "look the part" or because there are plans to use someone else. We must be very careful in doing God's business not to "hand pick" people based on our selfish needs and preferences.

By the same token, one cannot (should not) put others into ministry offices just because he or she feels they are capable — without knowing from those individuals whether God has called them to a particular office or not.

And he gave some, apostles; and some prophets; and some, evangelists; and some, pastors and teachers;

For the perfecting of the saints, for the work of the ministry, for the edifying of the body of Christ:

***Till we all come in the unity of the faith,* and of the knowledge of the Son of God, unto a perfect man, unto the measure of the stature of the fullness of Christ** [See also 1 Corinthians 12:27,28].
Ephesians 4:11-13

There are three reasons why God placed the fivefold ministries (apostles, prophets, evangelists, pastors, and teachers) in the church. They are:

1. For the perfecting **(completeness)** of the saints.

2. For the work **(formation and effective delivery)** of the ministry.

3. For the edifying or building up of the body of Christ.

God placed these ministries in the church for its physical and spiritual development, for its maturity. He places these ministries in those whom He sees fit as it suits Him. Appearance, status, background, education, and so on have nothing to do with it. The phrase "until we all come into the unity of the faith" describes an on-going effort of God — through those whom He has gifted — to bring the body of Christ into one belief. There will be an on-going effort to "come into the unity of the faith" right up until the catching away of the people of God; especially because so many ungodly things have infiltrated and permeated not only society, but the church. Sin is on the rise!

Therefore, it is important for us to understand that these ministry gifts will always be needed in the body of Christ. They are to help us become more Christ-like, more God-focused. "He must become greater; I (we) must become less" (John 3:30 NIV). The ministry gifts were designed by God to be self-less (or non-selfish) ways to help others grow in Christ. They have nothing to do with "self". It is all about what God wants for His people. These gifts must be governed by God and not by man. Therefore, we must be sensitive to the Holy Spirit and to the gifts that God has placed in each of us. It is important that those who operate in the fivefold ministry gifts hate the things that God hates and love the things that God loves because it is only then that the church will begin to move toward unity and become more effective.

Here are some important things to remember about ministry:

• God does the calling and placing in the "body" as it pleases Him.

• You should go into ministry because you know God called you. Know the "divine call" upon your life as the Holy Spirit bears witness with your spirit. You will be spiritually equipped with the gifts of the Spirit — as God sees fit — that will enhance and accompany the office to which you are called.

• God speaks to the "inner person" or heart, not the mind! Your mind will play tricks on you. Listen to the voice of God in your heart.

• Be sure to answer the call. Knowing that you are called is not enough. You must *respond* to that call with a verbal confession and acceptance of it. You must also be obedient and faithful to that calling on your life in order to experience a personal fulfillment in God.

• God will confirm His call on your life at some point and time. Don't put your time limits on God, it won't work.

• There are many workers in the body of Christ who fill whatever "vacancies" there are. However, one must come to a place where he or she knows God's specific purpose for him or her. Simply filling a need does not mean one is actually "called" to a particular office. In other words, just because you fill a need in your local church does not mean God has called you to that office. You are simply filling in until God sends in, or raises up, that one who is called to that office. You must be willing to recognize this.

Don't get me wrong. I believe that God honors those who are willing to work. There are times when local assemblies may not have the necessary workers who are "called" to specific ministries, and they simply use who they have until God sends in more workers. Even so, sometimes there are those who are called to specific ministries but are not willing to work, for whatever reason. God will raise up others to do the work if these individuals don't want to work!

I believe that when it comes to the fivefold ministries, there should be no "substitutes" (those who aren't called by God to these specific areas). These offices are far too important to the body of Christ for "substitutes!" Don't let anyone put you in an office God has not called you to! For example, I would not want to perform surgery on anyone because I am not schooled to be a surgeon. Therefore, if I tried to function as a surgeon I would do more harm to an individual than good. This might be an extreme example; nonetheless, I think you get the point. Even in the natural realm, people usually try to stick to their profession (an area or areas that they have expertise in or have been schooled for). Why should it be any different with the things of God? Let God do the calling, appointing, and anointing!

• The anointing accompanies one in ministry. In other words, the anointing comes upon the individual as he or she stands in that office to minister. One operating under the anointing, can distinguish the difference as opposed to operating within his or her own scope of ability. The anointing causes one to "minister" in a specific area and in ways that effectively touch and change the lives of the recipients. The best way that I can describe it is by saying it is a supernatural occurrence.

In other words, the anointing causes one to know what the mind and will of God is — for that moment — for a particular group of people or individual. The anointing gives one insight in the spirit realm and causes him or her to operate in that arena to fulfill and bring about — through the power of God — God's desired end for that group of people or individual.

• Let God specify and outline the parameters in which you should operate.

• Ministry goes beyond head knowledge! Ministry doesn't necessarily or always require "formal training." It is up to the individual and God.

When God summons you, He is "calling you forth." He is calling you to *do* something. A "call" demands action in response. A charge is never given for one to be at a standstill. It is given so that one can use his or her resources to move forward in a *specific direction* with the purpose of accomplishing something. With a call come obligations. It requires obedience and personal commitment from the one who is called. It requires complete trust in the Word of God regardless of how impossible that "call" may seem.

One should strive to know the voice of God better, for example, than Samuel did as a child. During Samuel's early years of training under Eli to "minister before the Lord," he did not know God's voice. It took him a while to recognize the voice of God. In fact, when God first spoke to Samuel, he answered Eli, thinking it was he who called him. After the third time, Eli finally realized it was God calling Samuel and instructed him that the next time he heard the voice he should answer, "Speak, Lord, for your servant is listening" (1 Samuel 3:1-10 NIV).

Samuel didn't know God's voice because the Word of God had not yet been revealed to him (1 Samuel 3:7).

Samuel was placed in the position to "minister before the Lord" by his mother Hannah who promised God that if He gave her a son, she would give him back to God to serve Him all the days of his life (1 Samuel 1:11). So Samuel's position started out as a down payment of a vow made by his mother. Yet he had to get acquainted with the God that his mother knew and trust in Him for himself.

A call demands readiness and responsiveness. God wants to pour out His Spirit on all flesh in these last days (Joel 2:28,29, Acts 2:17,18). He wants us to experience a visible, tangible manifestation of His power. God is waiting for those who are called by His name to take a stand and answer the "call". He is looking for those who are willing and obedient and who will fulfill His purpose here on earth. He is looking for willing workers in His kingdom, those who will say "yes" to Him. As Jesus sent out the seventy-two other disciples by twos, He said to them,

> **"Go! I am sending you out like lambs among wolves.**
>
> **Do not take a purse or bag or sandals; and do not greet anyone on the road."**
>
> **Luke 10:3,4 (NIV)**

Remember Jonah? God called him to preach to the Ninevites. God even gave him the specific words to speak. Yet he rejected God's call at first. But after going through a severe test, he answered the call when it was made the second time.

Remember Peter? God had to prepare him to answer the call that would come from Cornelius through his two servants. God showed Peter a vision of all kinds of four-footed animals on a large sheet and told Peter to get up, kill, and eat. Peter, not knowing what the ultimate purpose and message of this vision meant, responded, "I have never eaten anything impure or unclean" (Acts 10:9-14 NIV). God gave him the opportunity three times to eat any of the animals he chose, but his response was the same each time.

Ultimately, Peter got the message. God was preparing him and calling him to share the Gospel to men and women no matter what their nationality was. In this particular case, it was to share his knowledge of Christ, his experience as a Christian, and to offer salvation to Cornelius — the Gentile — and his household. Peter's problem was that he was bound to Jewish tradition and law. How many of us are bound to traditions and laws that God no longer has respect for? For example, the Mosaic laws given to the children of Israel by Moses were specifically for the children of Israel. But under the "new covenant" or New Testament, God did away with *some* of those laws through Christ Jesus. This by no means gives us a license to sin because the things that God wants us to strictly adhere to are repeated in the New Testament (e.g. — The Ten Commandments, see Romans 13:8,9). Nine of the Ten Commandments are taught in the New Testament (all except the Sabbath which was an observance for the Jews only under the Old Testament laws — see Exodus 31:14-17. Jesus Christ is the end of works. He is the Sabbath rest for all believers (Hebrews 4:9,10). This was exactly why God showed Peter the vision. It was to prepare his heart to receive and minister to a Gentile and his household, even though Jewish law forbade him to do so. We have got to go beyond our own perceptions and let God lead us, if we are going to win a dying world for Christ.

Peter's obedience and answer to the call resulted in the outpouring of the Holy Spirit upon Cornelius and his household. Afterward, they were baptized in water — signifying burial with Christ, removal of sins, and newness of life in Christ.

Abraham answered the call when God spoke to him and said, "...Leave your country, your people and your father's household and go to the land I will show you" (Genesis 12:1 NIV). He ventured out on God's instruction and received many blessings because of his obedience and answer to the call of God. I'm not saying this was an easy thing to do; but nonetheless, Abraham obeyed because he knew the voice of God and trusted Him. As a result of his obedience and faith in God, he was blessed with earthly possessions, he was in covenant relationship with God, he became the "father of many nations," and he and Sarah brought forth the promised seed (Isaac) in their old age.

Noah answered the call when God instructed him to build an ark. He moved on God's specific instructions and timeline. As a result of obeying God's call, Noah and his household were saved along with the animals that he separated for the ark.

Just like in the days of Noah, there may be people around you who think you are crazy because God has placed a call on your life that might appear "out of the norm," "out of season," or does not seemingly fit your character, yet you dare to believe God. Remember, it is much better to obey God. Heed the call, sister; it could mean the difference between life and death for you and others.

God doesn't operate in our time frame; neither does He think like we do. He will speak a word to you that will seem "out of season," crazy, and even impossible to you, but God knows exactly what He is doing. He is never out of season; He's right on time!

See Exodus chapters 28 and 31:1-5 for details on how God "called" Aaron to the priesthood as well as characteristics and qualifications that were necessary before one could be called to such a position.

Public and Private Call

Some of us are called publicly, and some of us are called privately.

Public — "The community or the people as a whole. A group of people sharing a common interest."[2]

Private —"Secluded from the sight, presence, or *intrusion* of others. Of or confined to one person; *personal.*"[3]

Let me explain. To be called "publicly" simply means that God has called you forth in a public setting, around others who you share a common interest with. This call is usually given to you through someone else who God chooses to use (e.g., a prophet). In most cases — in this type of setting — others also benefit because they hear God's specific purpose for you, making them witnesses. This is a good opportunity for others to begin to pray on your behalf and to be supportive as God takes you through the process of preparation for whatever that "call" is.

I believe God does this public calling so that, as the individual begins to fulfill that purpose or step into that office, others will know of a surety that God did it and no one else. In addition, others will witness that which God said He would do. To the one being called out, this may actually cause a bit of anxiety because now, others know and will sometimes begin to press that individual for him or her to begin to operate in the area God called him or her to — before it's actually time. *This is not God's will.*

There is always a time of preparation, a growing process. Only God knows when that individual is ready to move forward. Only He knows how long or short the preparation time should be.

A "private call" is when God speaks to you in your spirit; sometimes when no one else is around. It is a personal call that is only meant for you to know for a given time. One can be "privately called" during his or her personal study of the Bible or during his or her prayer and meditation time — the time when one reflects on the Word of God and listens for the voice of God. God can also "call" one privately in a public setting. This "call" takes place in the heart (spirit) of an individual. That is, God speaks quietly to you and you alone.

The difference between a "private call" and a "public call" is that God speaks to the inner person when privately calling one. He can also speak "privately" through the teaching or preaching of the Word. Something said could quicken in your spirit and be a confirmation of what God has already told you. You can also receive a prophetic word privately in a public setting.

Whether you are called "publicly" or "privately," the Word of God is sure. It will come to pass.

"For the revelation awaits an appointed time; it speaks of the end and will not prove false. Though it linger, wait for it; it will certainly come and will not delay."

Habakkuk 2:3 (NIV)

"Wait" in this context actually means "To be prepared or ready."[4] It means to continue working and, at the same time, begin to prepare yourself for that which God has spoken to you, until the time has "fully come" or until His Word is fulfilled in you.

My Call To Preach
The First Call

On June 29, 1997, the women of Bethel Tabernacle Pentecostal Church in Boston, Massachusetts gathered together on a Sunday afternoon for their first Virtuous Women's service. I remember it was a warm summer day. We all anticipated a mighty move of God through the speaker, who had already delivered a word from God that morning. Just as we anticipated, God moved mightily in the afternoon service. The woman of God challenged us to be more in God and to "rise to the occasion" — so to speak — in the things that God was calling us to. It was one of those services that caused me to evaluate my spiritual life and really focus on my purpose. What is my purpose now? What will it become in the future? How will it unfold?

At the end of the message, the woman of God called for all the women who recognized that God was doing something greater in their lives, to come forward for prayer. Needless to say, a long prayer line formed, of which I was a part. In fact, I remember vividly, as if it were yesterday, that I was about the third to the last person in the line for prayer. The woman of God laid hands on everyone as God led her. Prophecy went forth to some of the women, and I was charged up because I always get excited when I see God using other people and speaking a word into their lives. Finally it was my turn to receive prayer. I was ready — so I thought. My hands were raised, eyes closed; I believe I was even praying in tongues at first. The woman of God laid hands on me and began to pray, "You have been anointed to do what you are doing. God wants to take you to another level."

By now I was no longer praying in tongues or in English. I was silent with my hands raised and eyes closed just listening. She went on to say, "God has called you to preach. Everything that you've gone through was necessary in order for God to use you. God can't use anything He hasn't tested. You will stand out in this church. When people look at you, you'll be the example of praise."

After this, she began to pray in tongues, laying hands on me, and I began to pray in tongues. But while all of this was happening, in my mind I was substituting the word "preach" with "teach." You see, I already knew that God called me to teach — and was already teaching — because God revealed it to me. He "privately" called me to teach and then publicly confirmed it months later. I kept thinking, she didn't mean "preach" she meant "teach." She made a mistake and said "preach." At the time, the word "preach" made me feel overwhelmed and anxious.

As I usually do when I receive a prophetic word, I write it down word for word in a journal and wait for God to confirm it in my spirit and bring it to pass, if He has not already done so. So I went home that night and began writing in my journal everything that the woman of God said to me that afternoon. But something happened as I was writing. I decided that she could not have said "preach;" she meant "teach;" therefore, I stopped writing and instead, threw out what I had already written. I realized later that I did this because I was running away from the call. I did not want to preach, didn't ask God for it, wasn't accepting it, and that settled it! At least, so I thought.

Instead of having peace of mind about all of this, I became very burdened. I thought that I had settled the fact that God didn't call me to preach, yet everyday it was on my mind. Part of the reason that I felt burdened was because God had not confirmed the call to preach in my spirit. I was not convinced that this was what He wanted me to do. I also felt burdened and rejected the call to preach because at the time, when I thought about "preach-ing," I thought about a certain style of delivering God's Word that I had grown accustomed to and I knew that par-ticular style was not for me. I began to pray, seeking God's direction and confirmation in my spirit, but it just didn't happen. A couple of months went by, and I was more bur-dened than ever. Nevertheless, I went on with my life allowing God to use me in the areas He had already con-firmed in my spirit.

The Second Call

On Friday night, August 29, 1997, the Annual Jubilee Convention was in progress at Bethel Tabernacle Pente-costal Church. I had been anticipating this event all year because I always have a good time at the Jubilee services. There were guest speakers arriving from North Carolina and Indiana. That night the man of God preached a power-ful message. Excitement was in the air. The young people were charged up. Above all, God was moving.

Almost inevitably, everyone expects that at the end of a sermon there will be an altar call (for sinners) and/or a prayer line (for saints). That particular night, however, there was no altar call or prayer line (until much later). I remem-ber standing up — as many others did — and feeling abso-lutely charged up in the spirit, wondering what was going to happen next. All of a sudden, the man of God pointed to me and said, "You, come here." You can imagine how I felt because the church was filled with saints, and I was being put on the spot. I looked at him, put my finger on my chest and motioned with my lips "Me?" he said "Yes, you." As I stepped out into the aisle and walked to the front of the church, I thought, "This can't be happening to me. Why is he calling me out?" I went and stood before the preacher with my eyes closed. A host of other ministers were standing there to assist the preacher. I raised my hands as I always do in reverence to God.

The preacher began to say, "You're struggling with those gifts. God has anointed you, He has gifted you. You can't help it that you're gifted. They are trying to hold you back." The last statement of this prophetic word alerted me to the fact that the preacher was referring to those in the body of Christ when he said "they." However, I believe "they" not only speaks of those in the body of Christ, but also of demonic forces that will try to hinder the work of God through me. Those weapons won't prosper! In fact, the latter part of the preacher's prophecy was confirmed to me in the spirit realm and through certain experiences that, in fact, had already occurred but were now more recognizable and easily discerned because of this part of the prophecy.

He (the preacher) went on to say, "God has ordained you from your mother's womb, and He is calling you to preach." I had my eyes closed very tight and my teeth were clenched together because I could not believe what he was saying to me, and I was uncomfortable standing before all those people, all of whom heard (if they were listening) the prophetic words that he spoke to me. This was a "public call." All I wanted to do was get back to my seat in a hurry. In addition, the same preacher that prophesied to me back in June for our women's ministry service was one of the ministers standing by listening to every word that this man of God was saying. She remembered her prophecy to me because I spoke with her briefly at the conclusion of that service. The prophecy this night was an absolute confirmation to everything she (the evangelist) had said to me two months earlier. Boy, was I feeling overwhelmed!

The preacher went on to say, "When I lay my hands on you, your ministry will be released." He laid hands on me and began to charge me and empower me through the leading of God, and it seemed like all of the ministers standing around were on one accord with him; everyone was praying and agreeing with the man of God except me. I felt immobile. I couldn't say a word but just stood there with my eyes closed and hands raised. This "call" was too great for me. I remember hearing the voice of my pastor say, "Open your mouth!" As in, give God praise, and I did, mostly out of obedience.

After this was all over, I went back to my seat, and God continued to move through the service with healing and deliverance, but I struggled with the word I had received.

From that point on, I began to give in a little, and I told God that however He wanted to use me would be fine with me. I had been yielding to God all along (even before receiving the prophecies). I just didn't think He would call me to preach! Why was I having such a hard time with this? Because I felt undeserving of such an awesome task. I felt too "ordinary" for such a task as this and, quite frankly, didn't want such task. I felt unequipped, and I feared the unknown about preaching. What would it be like? Would I say the right things? How would I organize a sermon? The questions went on and on in my head. I even tried to convince God that I was not worthy of such a call to ministry and that He should choose someone else (like Moses did), but He didn't. He chose me and eventually I would have to accept the call, answer to it, and begin to prepare myself for it.

I barely wanted to talk with anyone about this and didn't. On the other hand, many already knew about it because both prophecies were given to me publicly. For many reasons now, I'm glad that God called me to ministry that way (publicly).

From September 1997 to May 1998, I committed myself to prayer and fasting on behalf of the call to preach. In fact, I took advantage of the month of consecration at my church (January 1998) to petition God and to listen for His voice concerning this preaching ministry. For the entire month of January, I heard nothing from God about preaching. I could sense Him strengthening other areas of ministry and gifts in my life but nothing about preaching. I decided that I had already petitioned God enough and would just continue doing the work of the Lord until He decided it was time to speak to me. During this interim, I had very few conversations with others about this. I primarily spoke only to one or two people who were called to preach most recently, with the exception of one other person who has been in ministry for many years. I wanted to get this person's perspective and hear of the experiences this individual had when called to a preaching ministry.

One thing that was unanimous among those I spoke with, was that they all agreed that prophecy should be a confirmation of what God has already revealed to an individual. This is a truth that I've always lived by. Suddenly I realized why I was so burdened. I am accustomed to God speaking directly to me first (my inner person) and then sending confirmation afterward. This time — the first time I had experienced it this way — He sent prophecy first. This created tremendous stress and anxiety in me. I also believe that I was having difficulty with this call to preach because I had other priorities in my life and felt that God picked the worst time to call me to this kind of ministry. I later repented for having felt that way. God's time is always the right time!

When God placed certain spiritual gifts in my life, He spoke directly to me. I had an unction, an urge, an inward witness. For example, when He called me to teach in October 1995, He spoke directly to my spirit. I remember sitting in my living room in Brockton, Massachusetts. I had taken the day off from work to get some things done, and while sitting at home, a voice — the voice of God — said to me, as plain as anything, "You're going to teach." Just like that. Notice,

God did not ask me if I wanted to teach. There was no choice in the matter. He told me, "You're going to teach." I remember the excitement I felt in my spirit, and I also remember looking around in the living room as if someone else was present with me. That's how clear God's voice was. I immediately began to praise God for the word He had spoken into my life. I knew without a shadow of a doubt that this word would come to pass because God said it.

God later confirmed His call to teach on my life through a dear friend — whom I had not shared this with — in the summer of 1996. I remember being in church that Sunday morning, and the evangelist was ministering through the prophetic anointing that God placed on her life. Many saints had gotten in the prayer line, including myself. I was the last person in the line, and as I prayerfully watched and listened to the woman of God minister to those before me, I prayed an inward prayer and asked God to confirm His call on my life to teach through this evangelist. I had done so not because I doubted God, but because I wanted to experience the awesomeness of God's ability not only to hear, but to answer prayer yet another time.

When it was my turn to be prayed for, as usual, I moved forward with uplifted hands and eyes closed in total worship of my God. She began to pray for me but suddenly stopped and started prophesying (speaking the divine utterance of God for my life) directly to me. What do you think God had His servant say to me? You guessed it! She began to confirm the call to teach that God had placed on my life. At the time, I could hardly contain myself because God had answered my prayer. He's an awesome God! He sent confirmation, and I was (and still am) excited about what God was/is doing in my life.

There are other gifts that God has placed in my life that I'm aware of because He revealed them to *me.* So you see, I had grown accustomed to God speaking to me first and then confirming it through others. At this point, even if God never confirmed — through others — the gifts and ministries He had already placed in my life, it wouldn't matter to me because He had already spoken to me and I knew He would bring it to pass.

Somehow though "the call to preach" was different. God chose to go a different route. Trying to figure out the mind of God is no easy task. But I've learned over the years that God knows exactly what He's doing. You may not understand what God is doing in your life right away; but if you continue to move in the direction He is taking you, love Him, and serve Him wholeheartedly; He will unfold — in due time — His plan for your life.

The Third Call

By May 1998, I was no longer burdened about the call to preach. I stopped thinking and talking about it. I felt myself growing spiritually. God was working in my life. I had reached a level of excitement about what God was (and still is) doing in my life and in the lives of others. It seemed that my whole attitude had changed. It's not as if I wasn't excited about serving God before, but there was a special aura of excitement and calmness in my spirit that wasn't there ten months previous. At that point, I had *totally* yielded to God, meaning that *whatever* He was doing in my life was alright with me.

On May 7, 1998, the youth department at my church hosted a youth revival. They invited a guest speaker from New Jersey to minister the Word of God during the three-day revival. Again, I was charged up and looked forward to the services. I anticipated a mighty move of God. Never get God's attention or get into His presence without expecting something great! I went to church that night knowing that we would receive from God's Word, and we certainly did.

The woman of God presented the Word graciously and with personal conviction. She not only spoke from the Word of God, but she shared a lot out of her own experiences. My heart was open and receptive to God throughout the service. She stated how God had impressed upon her to challenge His people to a higher level and, that, she did. She challenged us to come out of our comfort zone and move to the next level in God. That word "next level" stuck with me. As she shared that night I began to examine my life as a believer, and I can remember speaking to God inwardly and saying, "Lord I want to be in your divine will. I want to serve you better than I've been serving you. Whatever you want me to do, I'll do." I felt relieved inside. As the preacher was closing out her message, I remember raising my hands to God and surrendering completely to Him.

The woman of God concluded her sermon by asking everyone in the building to seriously consider the things that God was doing in their lives. But she went beyond that. She asked everyone who was willing to admit that God was taking them to another level — and wanted to accept the challenge — to move out of the pews and fill the altar. She specifically asked these individuals to raise their hands in submission and worship to God. Without hesitation, I stepped out into the aisle — hands raised — and made my way toward the altar. Tears were streaming down my face as I paced the floor that night. At that point I was completely "broken." All I wanted to do was to please God. I knew in my spirit that I had accepted the call to preach. I just knew it! I felt an intensity of the presence of God in my spirit. One thing I should make clear before I go any further is that there was never a doubt in my mind that God had spoken through the three individuals to me. My struggle was not with their credibility as servants of God or with God; it was with myself and what I had become accustomed to. Don't look for God to speak to you always in the same way. He may come from another direction, and you could miss your blessing.

As I reached the front of the church — looking at no one and feeling totally overwhelmed by the presence of God — the woman of God began to beckon to me. I could hear her saying softly, "You, come here." She was even pointing her finger at me. The altar was filled with men and women who had come forward to accept the challenge God placed on them. Somehow though, I was the one being called out again. I remember being amazed — yet another time — that I was being called out in the midst of many others.

As I approached the woman of God who was still standing behind the pulpit, I began to pray in tongues. This time felt *different* for me than at other times. She literally poured anointing oil in the palm of her hands and saturated both of my hands with oil. I believe — through the divine leading of God — this woman was anointing (consecrating) me for the office of a preacher. Similar to what Samuel did to David when he anointed him king over Israel. My hands had enough oil to grease the ashiest skin. She did not do a whole lot of loud praying. In fact, she prayed very softly, and I could barely hear what she was saying. Suddenly, she said to me in a calm, soft, confident, assuring, peaceable, God-inspired tone, "Just say yes. God just wants you to say yes."

Well, without hesitation I said, "Yes, Yes, Yes" over and over again, and I stepped down from the pulpit area. I had a sense that all eyes were now on me to see what was going on, but I kept my eyes on God and continued worshipping Him. I had already accepted the call to preach even before she called me out. Nevertheless, God had it so ordained that His maidservant would travel miles to minister directly to me, letting me know that everything God is doing in me is all right, and all I need to do is *trust Him* and give a *positive response* to the call. From that moment on, I've experienced an indescribable peace within — the peace of God that passes all understanding. The burden that I had carried up to that point had lifted, and I felt a "blessed assurance" inside. What a mighty God we serve!

Although it was a month or two later before I shared with anyone (except my husband) that I had accepted the call to preach, I felt at peace with God and myself. At the time, it didn't matter to me if anyone else ever knew. I was experiencing such a sense of relief and peace; I just wanted to bask in it for a while before saying anything to anyone.

No longer am I concerned — or anxious for that matter — about what I will be like as a preacher. God called me; He will establish me in due time.

Being confident of this very thing, that he which hath begun a good work in you will perform *it* until the day of Jesus Christ.

Philippians 1:6

On Saturday, September 12, 1998, I attended a revival service sponsored by the men's ministry at my church. God began to speak to me directly during the "praise and worship" portion of the service. Finally, He confirmed in my spirit the "call to preach." He said, "There's a *word* over your head...That word shall be confirmed. You shall go forth in ministry; *you shall declare the Word of the Lord!*" The Spirit of the Lord then led me to lay hands on myself to fortify and charge (energize) myself as I continued to receive what He was saying to me. I am so glad that God is mindful of me. I am forever grateful that He took the time to minister directly to me concerning the task that He has placed in my hands.

Perhaps my experience will help you as you accept the challenge God has placed in your life, whatever it is. Looking back at my experiences, I often wonder if I would have accepted the call to preach any more easily if God had spoken directly to me first. I don't know that I would have, but I'm thankful now for having gone through the process. My sister, put your trust in God. He will not give you more than you can handle; He loves you too much.

Be encouraged; God will not leave you without a word. Just be patient and trust Him because He knows exactly what He is doing.

[1]*The American Heritage Dictionary,* p. 99.
[2]*The Merriam Webster Dictionary,* p. 590.
[3]*The Merriam Webster Dictionary,* p. 580.
[4]*The American Heritage Dictionary,* p. 820.

Chapter 7
The Blessing

The Bible teaches us that life and death are in the power of the tongue (Proverbs 18:21). It also teaches us that we are snared by the words of our mouth (Proverbs 6:2). I opened this chapter with these truths because it is important for us to understand that our words have power! We can produce either blessings or curses in our lives based on what we confess. Sometimes we forget this, and we walk around confessing things like, "I am broke" or "I'm always sick." These statements may be true, but as believers, we need to confess the desired end result of a situation, not what presently is. So instead of saying, "I am broke," we should confess, "I am financially stable, secure, and blessed!" Instead of saying, "I'm always sick," we should confess, "Christ died for my continual healing, and because of this, I am healthy. All root of sickness in me is dried up and cursed by the blood of Jesus, and I have no more symptoms."

I used the above examples because they seem to be the areas that believers struggle with the most: finances and health. These are general examples of how we snare (trap, limit) and curse (invoke evil upon) ourselves because we don't take time to organize our words, based on the Word of God, before we speak. Remember, the Bible teaches that whatever comes out of the mouth is really coming from the heart. "...for out of the abundance of the heart the mouth speaketh" (Matthew 12:34). This is an indication that what we say is what we believe and, in most cases, what we know. However, there is a principle at work that every believer should grasp hold to and that is, it doesn't matter what appears to be or what we feel. What matters is what God speaks on our behalf. In fact, Jesus said that He not only came to give life but to give it more abundantly (John 10:10). This means that if we are going to be a blessed people, we must walk in the words of life that Jesus spoke on our behalf.

As Christians, we cannot walk by what we see or feel. "The just shall live by faith" (See Habakkuk 2:4). What does this mean? The believer's victory or the outcome of our circumstance is not based on what presently exists; neither is it based on the natural realm (what we see, think, or feel), although our circumstances involve the natural realm. Things may not look good now, but that doesn't mean it will always be that way. Because you are broke now, does not mean that God can't turn things around for you and cause you to prosper in the future. The only way that you can be in the situation you're in, yet know that God will turn things around for you, is through the eyes of faith. Faith says, "I don't have any money now, but tomorrow is a new day with new blessings and mercies; therefore, my needs (and wants, provided I delight myself in the Lord) will be met each and every day above my expectations." In other words, we should confess our needs and wants as if they are already provided for, because in fact, they are!

We can look at this as a "kingdom principle." Speak your desired end! I am rich in Christ Jesus because I am an heir and joint-heir with Him. I am healed by the beatings and punishment Christ took for me. I took the time to share this information with you so that your heart will be prepared to receive the blessings of the Lord as He has laid it on my heart concerning you. Now, let's look at the word "blessing."

Blessing — "The act of one who blesses. An expression or utterance of good wishes. A special favor granted by God. *Something promoting or contributing to happiness, well-being, or prosperity.*"[1]

Notice, one of the definitions for "blessing" clearly says that to be blessed is to be happy, to prosper, and to have well-being. So, according to the definition, anything contrary to this is not considered a blessing. One who professes to be "blessed" should be happy, secure, sure, and constantly waiting with anticipation for God's Word to be fulfilled in his or her life. How can I say this? Does this mean that as Christians we will always be happy and never experience difficulties? No. On the contrary, many of us have already experienced much difficulty in life and have not always been happy or even victorious. Nonetheless, the Word of God says,

The blessing of the Lord brings wealth, and he adds no trouble to it.
Proverbs 10:22 (NIV)

As Christians, we know that it is God that contributes to our happiness, well-being, and prosperity. Being "sons of God" and not "bastards," gives us the right to celebrate and enjoy — keeping "things" in perspective — the abundant life (both spiritually and naturally) that Jesus Christ died that might obtain (John 10:10, 1 John 3:1,2, Hebrews 12:6-8). In addition, we know that "the blessing of the Lord" has a far greater meaning, relates to, and implies more than just earthly wealth, riches, or gain. God's plan for us is not a "get rich quick" scheme, and we should not deceive ourselves into believing this. Before blessings, comes tests, trials, and sufferings. Nonetheless, our blessings come from the Lord, and even when we do not feel or look blessed, we are still blessed! After we have proven ourselves faithful to God and to His Word, then He will release an overflow of blessings on and around us according to His will for our lives.

When we get to the place that no matter what presently exists, we can stand on the truth of the Word; then we will begin to experience the blessing of the Lord. When we can press beyond what we see and feel, and, instead of confessing what appears, train our hearts to believe and receive the Word of God, thereby confessing what it speaks on our behalf, then we will experience the blessing of the Lord.

Note that the blessing of the Lord is always present and available to all believers. Sometimes, however, we hold up our blessing because we are not in right standing with God or our lives don't measure up to the Word of God. Nonetheless, the blessing is always hovering, waiting for us to get ourselves in line with God's Word and receive it. It is important to know that in order to be blessed, we must follow the teachings of the Word of God. We cannot live as *we* please and expect God to bless us. What do I mean by this? We cannot serve God on Sunday and the devil Monday through Saturday and expect to receive God's blessings. We must live for God and obey His Word. We must live holy to the best of our ability, and after we've done all the Word of God instructs, we must simply STAND.

We cannot be compromising Christians when it comes to the Word of God. For example, if the Word of God says that in order for humankind to see (gain access to) the kingdom of God, one must be born again — of the water (baptism) and of the Spirit (be filled with the Holy Spirit), — then that's exactly how we must do it. (See John 3:3-6, Romans 8:1,2,5-11,13, Acts 2:38,39,41, Acts 4:8-12; 8:35-38, 18:8; 22:16, Philippians 2:9-11, Romans 6:1-4, Colossians 2:12, Galatians 3:27, 1 Corinthians 12:13, Mark 16:16).

Spirit breeds spirit, and flesh breeds flesh. If you want a spiritual blessing that will spill over into the natural realm of your life, then you must sow to the spirit realm (Ephesians 1:3,4). Another principle is at work when we talk about sowing. One never sows without reaping something in return. That's a biblical principle and truth. The Bible declares that we will reap what we sow. It also lets us know that if we sow to our flesh, we will reap corruption by the flesh, but if we sow to the Spirit, we will reap everlasting life by the same Spirit (Galatians 6:7,8). By the same token, if we sow sparingly, we will reap sparingly. So what does it mean to sow, and what does it mean to reap?

Sow — "To plant (seeds) to produce a crop. To scatter with or as if with seed. To spread."[2]

The seed of the believer is the Word of God. When you sow (sprinkle or spread) the Word of God into your life, you are planting whatever type of seed is needed (e.g., seed of salvation, seed of deliverance, seed of repentance, seed of forgiveness, seed of faith, and so on) in hopes (expectation) that that particular seed will grow in due season — through continual watering of the Word — to produce of its kind.

Reap — "To cut and gather (grain or a similar crop). To gather a crop from harvest. To gain as a reward, especially as a result of effort."[3]

The "sow and reap" principle is that after we have planted, scattered, and spread the Word of God into our lives to obey its teachings, we can then gather those things that the seed (Word) has produced. Nothing sown produces immediately, but consistent and faithful attention to that seed planted, will eventually bring about results.

One may think that the reaping aspect is where the blessing comes in, but it is really the sowing aspect that will secure and determine what your blessing will be. The reaping aspect is only the visible/tangible manifestation of what you've sown. The truth is, once you have planted the seed, you have already ensured your blessing.

If we sow in faith, according to the Word of God and His will for our lives, it will bring forth blessings! What does this say to us? It says that if we need blessings in specific areas of our lives, then it would make sense for us to sow spiritually in those areas.

A blessing often implies something undeserved, not obtained by purchase — one cannot work for it — something unaffordable or even impossible to attain unless God intervenes. God expects us to enjoy every blessing He bestows on us. The blessing of the Lord does not cause sorrow or grief; it brings abundance and productivity. It makes one prosperous!

You may ask, "How can I be blessed?" Begin to sow (plant) the seed (Word of God) in your life, and you will see results, for it is God that gives the increase. He will water that seed in your life and cause it to bring forth after its kind. Remember, God's Word is sure, and it will never return void, but instead, it will accomplish that which it was sent to do.

You don't have to wait for the preaching or teaching of the Word or for someone to speak a word into your life in order to be blessed. Speak the Word of God in your own life and watch God bring it to pass. My sister, there is a word that speaks to every area of your life. Whatever your need is, search the Scriptures and pull out those verses that apply to your specific need(s) and begin to confess them daily. God will honor your faith in His Word, and blessings will overtake you.

In closing, my prayer of blessing for you in accordance with the Word of God is that you would experience the following: the freedom of God's Word, the joy in knowing Christ as your personal Savior, complete and total deliverance from *all* obstacles and hindrances that prevent you from becoming a mature Christian who walks in love and forgiveness toward humankind, clear direction of God's purpose and will for your life, and mental, emotional, and spiritual healing. I pray that from this day forward, all of the ministries, gifts, and abilities that God has placed in you will be used — "as the Spirit wills" and for His glory — for the completeness of the saints, for the work of the ministry, and for the edification of all believers.

"The Lord bless you and keep you;

the Lord make his face shine upon you and be gracious to you;

the Lord turn his face toward you and give you peace."

Numbers 6:24-26 (NIV)

[1]*The American Heritage Dictionary,* p. 74.

[2]*The American Heritage Dictionary,* p. 654.

[3]*The American Heritage Dictionary,* p. 573.

Chapter 8
An Invitation

If you are without Jesus Christ as your Lord and Savior, you can receive Him today. Jesus Christ wants to be a part of your life, but He is waiting for you to invite and welcome Him into your heart. He is the only one that can make a difference in your life. In fact, Christ is our life which means that without Him, we have no life. Without Him we remain separated from God and have no eternal security that we will one day reign with Christ. Whether you know it or not, there is life after death. It's called eternal life. You can either spend it with Christ or spend it burning in hell forever. Revelation 21:8 tells us about those who will spend eternity in hell. Heaven on the other hand was created for those who have received Jesus Christ and obey His commands which are found in the Bible. The Gospel of John 14:1-3 describe the heavenly home that those of us who receive Christ will partake of.

My sister, I beseech you to choose life in Christ. The decision is yours, you must make it. Don't be swayed by influences in your life and in society that *will* try to deter you from giving your life to Christ.

Many of you reading this book have made provisions in the natural realm on behalf of your retirement and even life insurance to ensure that things are taken care of once you leave this life. Well it's the same spiritually. You *must* make the necessary provisions in order to face eternity in peace and Jesus Christ outlined what those provisions are.

You must come to God through Him (See John 10:1-14). You must be born again (See John 3:1-7).

> **See, I set before you today life and prosperity, death and destruction.**
>
> **For I command you today to love the Lord your God, to walk in his ways, and to keep his commands, decrees and laws; then you will live and increase....**
>
> **But if your heart turns away and you are not obedient, and if you are drawn away to bow down to other gods and worship them,**
>
> **I declare to you this day that you will certainly be destroyed....**
>
> **...Now choose life, so that you...may live**
>
> **and that you may love the Lord your God, listen to his voice, and hold fast to him. For the Lord is your life....**
>
> **Deuteronomy 30:15-20 (NIV)**

You can obtain this life that I'm talking about, and be "born again." Salvation is made available to you through Jesus Christ. The good news is, you don't have to work for salvation; it is free! (Ephesians 2:4,5,8,9, Romans 6:1,2, Romans 10:9,10,13). You simply have to obey the Word of God.

Here are some of the important components by which, if you obey, you can and will obtain salvation. First and foremost, ask Jesus Christ to save you and to come into your heart, then repent.

•*Repent* — is to change one's mind or purpose; to regret — turn away from sin, your ways, and the ways of the world (Acts 2:38; 26:20, Luke 5:32; 13:3,5).

•*Be baptized* in the name of the Lord Jesus Christ. We are buried with Christ by water baptism; just as Christ was raised from the dead so are we "raised" out of the water of baptism to walk in th newness of life (See Romans 6:3-14). So then water baptism denotes a "newness" of life in Christ; it identifies one with Christ (Acts 4:8-12).

• *Be filled with the Spirit* of God (Acts 2:38, Ephesians 5:18, Romans 8:9, John 4:24, Joel 2:28, Matthew 3:11).

• *Obey God's Word* and *live a life of holiness* (1 Thessalonians 4:7, Hebrews 12:14, Leviticus 20:7, 2 Corinthians 7:1, Ephesians 4:24, 1 Peter 1:16, 2 Peter 3:11).

You may feel that you are living a "good" life and may therefore wonder why you need Jesus. Well, I'll give you some reasons why you need Him. You need Christ in order to have victory over sin. You may say, "I'm not doing anything wrong," "I'm a good person — I don't steal, lie, cheat, curse...." Yet the Bible teaches that we were all born in sin and shaped in iniquity (Psalm 51:5). The Bible also says that all have sinned and come short of the glory of God (Romans 3:23). The only way to eradicate sin in your life is by receiving Jesus Christ because it was Jesus Christ who died for your sins (1 Peter 3:18, Hebrews 9:11-14; 10:14). He took upon Himself the sins of the entire human race so that we would not have to live as servants to sin any longer (Romans 6:1-7). The choice is yours. Who will you serve? Will it be Christ or the god of this world, Satan? I hope and pray that you choose Jesus (Matthew 6:24, Luke 16:13).

You need Christ in order to gain access to heaven (John 10:7-11,25-28). Jesus offers salvation not only to eradicate your sins, but also to get you ready to face eternity. That is, life after death. Every person that ever lived will either live in peace with Christ (heaven), (See John 14:1-3, 1 Thessalonians 4:14-17), or be damned forever in the lake of fire (hell), (See Revelation 20:15). Did you know that if you are without Christ and His salvation plan and are not observing or obeying the teachings of the Bible, you are doomed for hell? But you can change that. You can change the direction of your life and your eternal destination.

Because I'm concerned about where you will spend eternity and want you to experience the love of God, I have included additional Scripture references at the end of this chapter that will point you to Jesus and answer your questions about salvation and being "born again." It is by no means an extensive list, but it's enough to get you started. It is my prayer that you will spend some time reading these Scriptures and that God would prick your heart and give you an understanding of them so that you can obey them.

The Bible warns us that in the "last days" — the age of apostasy — people will have a desire to hear, believe, and follow teachings that are pleasant to their ears as opposed to hearing and receiving the Bible as the absolute and complete truth (2 Timothy 4:3,4). Such an influence comes from the god of this world, Satan. This "influence" or "spirit" has cast an ungodly desire on those who reject Christ and has opened up a world of acceptance to any and everything that opposes the teachings of the Bible. Nonetheless, the Bible must be our ultimate guide to truth and practice, and we must use it as a guide to judge what we believe and do.

Today many non-Christians and, sadly, even so-called Christians ask, "What gives you the right to say that Jesus Christ is the way, the truth, and the life?" (John 14:6). Those of us who stand on the Word of God and its principles are being called bigots because we are devoted to the Bible to follow its teachings. We are called intolerant because we do not accept, follow, or live according to the mandates of society. Jesus said, however, that if we want to enter life, we must obey His commandments (Matthew 19:17, Ecclesiastes 12:13,14, 1 John 5:3, Revelation 14:12, Exodus 20:6, Psalm 78:7).

Receive Jesus today. You have nothing to lose but everything to gain. The Apostle Paul counted everything a loss to gain Christ, and he seemingly had everything this world could offer yet his heart's desire was to know Christ in an intimate way (Philippians 3:10). With Christ in your life, you can make it!

Additional Definitions and Scripture References on Salvation

Repentance — The basic meaning of repentance is "to turn around." One must turn from his or her sins and turn to Christ. Repentance is a free decision on the part of sinners. *References:* Isaiah 30:15, Matthew 3:1,2; 4:17; 18:3, Luke 5:32; 15:7, Acts 2:38; 8:22; 11:18, 2 Peter 3:9, Luke 24:47, Mark 1:4, Acts 20:21, 26:20, 2 Corinthians 7:10.

Water Baptism — We are buried with Christ through baptism. *References:* John 3:3-7; Acts 2:38; 22:16, Romans 6:3-7, 1 Peter 3:21, Colossians 2:11-13, Ephesians 4:5, Acts 19:4,5.

Holy Spirit — God is a Spirit (John 4:24). The work of the Holy Spirit is to convict us of sin, give aide or guide, comfort, come along side, reveal, help us in our weakness, intercede for us, and so on. *References:* Acts 2:4-13,31,38,39; 4:8,31; 6:3-5; 7:55; 8:14-17; 9:17,31; 10:44-47; 11:15-17; 13:9; 14:3; 15:8; 19:1-7, Ephesians 1:13,14; 3:16; 5:18, John 3:8; 14:15-18,26,27; 15:26,27, Romans 8:2,13-15,26,27, John 16:7-11, 1 Corinthians 2:4,12; 12:13, Luke 4:18,19; 11:13, Psalm 51:10-12; 143:10, Galatians 5:16-18,25, 1 Thessalonians 1:5, 2 Thessalonians 2:13, 1 Peter 1:2, 2 Colossians 1:22; 5:5.

General References to Salvation, Sin, and Eternal Life:

John 3:3,16

John 15:1-6

Romans 5:12-15,19-21

Romans 6:23

Romans 8:24,25

Romans 10:8-10

1 Corinthians 6:9-11

Philippians 2:12,13

1 Peter 1:23

1 John 2:24,25

1 John 3:5,6

1 John 5:11,12

1 John 5:17,18

2 John 1:9

Choose life today. Make Jesus your choice.

It is my heart's desire that you have been blessed and enlightened by reading this book. Share its content with someone else. Make a spiritual investment in someone else's life by giving them a copy of this book. Reach out and touch someone's life in a positive way.

May God richly bless you and yours.